PLAN YOUR SUCCESS

SEVEN STRATEGIES TO GET STARTED ON ANY GOAL, MANAGE SETBACKS, AND ACHIEVE STRATEGIC OBJECTIVES IN RECORD-BREAKING TIME

MICHAEL WU

LIGHTHOUSE
MEDIA & PUBLICATIONS

Published by Lighthouse Media & Publications Inc.

ISBN 978-1-7387155-4-1 (Ebook)

ISBN 978-1-7387155-5-8 (Paperback)

ISBN 978-1-7387155-6-5 (Hardcover)

ISBN 978-1-7387155-7-2 (Audiobook)

CONTENTS

INTRODUCTION

A goal without a plan is just a wish.

— ANTOINE DE SAINT-EXUPÉRY

There were once three fish that lived along a riverbank. The first was named "Plan Ahead," the second "Think Fast," and the third "Go With The Flow."

One day, Plan Ahead overheard a fisherman saying that he would be casting his net in the pond to catch some fish the next day. He immediately informed the others, made his preparations, and within a few hours, swam away downstream.

The two remaining fish looked to each other for advice. Think Fast said, "If the rumor is true, then I'm sure I'll think of something when the time comes." Go With The Flow shook his head and said, "I don't know what the fuss is about. Just enjoy your life and believe that everything will work out."

The next day came, and just as Plan Ahead had cautioned, the fisherman made his way to the river. He found two fat and healthy-looking fish upstream and cast his net. Both Think Fast and Go With The Flow were caught, but in a matter of seconds, Think Fast was able to roll over and pretend he was dead, so the fisherman released him back into the water.

Unfortunately, Go With The Flow never made it out of the net. He was served on a plate as supper, later that evening, to the fisherman and his guests.

How many times in your life have you waited for opportunities to fall on your lap, believing more in luck than your own agency? While there is some truth to "going with the flow" and allowing life to unfold naturally, the only way to reach your next level is to do something!

You may have seen a few stories here and there about the entrepreneurs that seem like overnight successes. The simplicity of their business models has caused many people to believe that starting a company is easy-peasy. They assume that within a few years, they too can become multi-millionaires. But sadly, this assumption is false, and there is no such thing as overnight success or shortcuts to becoming a millionaire.

Success is more predictable than you might think. How come? It is the result of careful planning and relentless hard work. This may sound like "old school" advice, but there is a reason why it has stood the test of time.

Just look at the strong men and women who have contributed to the progression of society, such as Carl Jung, Florence Nightingale, Albert Einstein, and Nelson Mandela. Even though they came from different parts of the world, and lived in different eras, they all had one thing in common: a clear, concise, and powerful vision. Armed with a vision, they were able to decide where most of their time, money, and energy were spent, which helped them execute their plans efficiently.

Being a new immigrant in Canada, and attempting to start a life with my family, was not an easy undertaking. Before arriving here more than 10 years ago, I had imagined that opportunities are everywhere—well, at least that's the Western dream that was sold to me. But, the reality was that since I was an immigrant, becoming successful was going to be tougher for me than for the ordinary Canadian.

I got rejected from countless jobs due to culture. It seemed like I was fighting a losing battle, but before giving up, I decided to change my mindset. That was the breakthrough that I needed to turn my life around. I decided to plan for success, rather than leave it up to chance. This meant I had to put together a vision and strategic plan to reduce risk and achieve my goals in the shortest amount of time.

Many years later, I run multiple successful businesses, and it is all thanks to the systems I built while planning for my success. Even though I have experienced setbacks along the way, none of them were able to deter me from my vision. It is now my mission to teach those who are on their journey of personal development how to plan for their success.

Similar to me, you might have a dream, such as losing weight, starting a business, pursuing a degree, or advancing in your career. But what you are missing are the practical strategies on how to achieve your dream. In the following eight chapters, you will learn how to define what you want, reflect on why you want it, and design action steps to execute and manage your plan. What's great is that you don't need to have any prior business or project management knowledge to follow these practical guidelines.

Before we look at the strategies, the first chapter will outline the benefits of having a plan, and why it increases your likelihood of success.

1

FAILING TO PLAN IS PLANNING TO FAIL

Without goals, and plans to reach them, you are like a ship that has set sail with no destination.

— FITZHUGH DODSON

WHY YOUR TIME IS GOLDEN

Time is an arbitrary number that only becomes valuable when you consider that your life is established in time.

For instance, nine months is just a time frame, until you recognize that it took nine months to form you in your mother's belly. Or what is the significance of 12 months? Isn't it just a representation of a year? Well, yes it is. But consider how many goals you can achieve in 12 months. Below are a few examples:

- Learn a new language.
- Reach your fitness goal.
- Start a new business.
- Develop a positive mindset.
- Replace a bad habit with a healthy one.
- Learn a new skill.

The fact that your life exists in time means that you only have X amount of years, months, weeks, days, and hours on this earth. When a day passes, you can never get it back, and this goes for any opportunity that you miss too!

People often say that time is the most precious commodity; more precious than money. They say this because unlike money, you can never make up the time you have wasted. And if time cannot be retrieved, then how you live each day matters.

Every decision that you make can either be a good or bad use of your time. For example, smoking a cigarette can relieve momentary stress or anxiety. But if you calculate the long-term outcomes of smoking, you will discover that it is an expensive habit and not a good use of your time. Not only does it burn a hole in your wallet, but it can also lead to the deterioration of health.

What often motivates you to make decisions is the promise of short- or long-term gratification. When you are seeking short-term gratification, you are looking for an instant release of pleasurable emotions. Think about the feeling you get after a few puffs of a cigarette, or how excited you feel after swiping your credit card on a purchase.

Even though bad decisions are a poor use of time, you may be motivated to make them anyway because they bring some kind of short-term gratification. What you need to know about human beings is that we are wired to avoid pain and run toward pleasure. Your actions and motivations in life, whether they are a good or bad use of your time, can make you feel good. This is why you find it so difficult to break bad habits even though you know how much they are hurting you.

To reclaim time, it is important to shift from making choices that produce short-term gratification to choices that yield long-term gratification. Yes, it is true, when you delay gratification, you will need to wait longer to feel accomplished. However, the benefit is that you get to make better choices, each day, that are productive and add value to your life.

Please realize that not every good choice feels good at the moment. For example, replacing a juicy hamburger meal for a chicken salad can feel underwhelming. Just imagine how much vitality you will feel in your body after a few months of making healthy food replacements. Good choices can sometimes feel boring, or require you to step outside of the comfort zone. It can take a while to adjust to healthy habits and eliminate unnecessary tasks from your calendar. However, the delayed gratification is worth it! In the long-term, you can look back and marvel at the goals you have achieved.

The strategies presented in this book won't bring immediate results because they require you to put in the work and commit the hours to practice. I can also guarantee you that you won't always feel motivated to implement these strategies and cut off habits that interfere with your progress. However, what I can say is that your commitment to working on these strategies is a good use of time! In the long run, you will reap the rewards of developing successful habits and executing your vision as diligently as possible.

You Only Need Three Hours

One of the excuses I hear often when people explain why they cannot pursue their goals is a lack of time. They tell me about their busy schedules, which don't allow for much free time. In response, I tell them that they will never have such a thing as "free time" because there is always something to be done. However, if they are serious about pursuing their goals, they will need to *find time* instead.

As a businessman running multiple businesses, I never have free time. But, when it comes to the things I value, such as my family, health, and career, I have to find the time. Every person is given the same 24 hours in a day, but how each of us spends our 24 hours will determine how well we manage our time.

Let's consider how the average person spends their time on a normal work week:

- Sleep = 8 hours
- Work = 9 hours
- Commuting = 2 hours
- Eating meals = 3 hours
- Socializing/spending time with family = 2 hours

With just five major daily tasks, the average person's 24 hours is used up. They have no free time because there is always something to be done. Nevertheless, the same person can find time, if they find ways to save it on their existing tasks.

For example, they might cut their commute time short by moving closer to work, negotiating a hybrid work schedule, or finding a quicker mode of transport. They can cut their eating time short by prepping meal ingredients in advance or taking turns cooking with their spouse or roommate.

Time spent socializing can also be cut short by scheduling video calls instead of one-on-one meetups, or socializing during meal times to complete two tasks at once. After making these adjustments, they might have three or more hours available to spend working on their goals.

Research shows that the average individual can remain productive for 3–4 hours (Escar, 2022). During these hours, your concentration is at its peak and you can enter a flow state (the state of being fully immersed in an experience that you lose track of time). You can maximize your productivity during those 3–4 hours by planning how you want to spend them; by making a list of tasks you will be focusing on.

Therefore, if you are like me, and many other working individuals who simply don't have time, adjust how you are currently spending your time, and find 3–4 hours to spend working on your goals. If 3–4 hours sounds like a lot, then even an hour will make a big improvement. But remember, the hour won't appear magically on your calendar—you need to find it!

THE IMPORTANCE OF PLANNING FOR SUCCESS

The majority of the time dedicated to working on your goals should be spent on planning. When most of your effort has been invested in the plan, the execution of it becomes straightforward. I learned this lesson early on when I was starting out as an entrepreneur. The more time I spent working on my business plan, the fewer mistakes I made while operating my business.

When explaining the process of problem-solving, Albert Einstein said, "If I had an hour to solve a problem, I'd spend 55 minutes thinking about the problem and 5 minutes thinking about solutions" (Debevoise, 2021). He was simply emphasizing the importance of preparation before pursuing any kind of goal. When you spend a significant amount of time researching a problem; understanding what it is and how it came about, you get to save more money and time solving it.

There are five reasons why you should always start a goal by creating a plan:

- **You will have a clear roadmap on where you are going**. Plans outline the objectives you want to accomplish, but most importantly, they give you a step-by-step guide on how you will go about doing it.
- **You will be more motivated.** When you are confident about where you are going and the steps you need to take, you can reduce the feeling of being overwhelmed by the journey, and organize each day around the goal-related tasks you need to complete.
- **You will spend time more efficiently**. Each step or task related to your goal takes a certain amount of hours, days, or months to complete. Having a plan can help you decide on the most important tasks to complete each day, and how much time to allocate to them.
- **You will solve problems quicker**. Creating a plan allows you to anticipate obstacles and carefully think about your options. When you run into problems in the future, you can refer back to your plan and take the necessary actions.

- **You will have a system to hold you accountable.** By nature, a plan has set expectations that you need to fulfill in order to move from one stage of your goal to another. A good plan will include several objectives and milestones that you can use to measure your progress and stay on track to completing your goal.

Creating a plan saves you a lot of time in the long run. Once you reach the point where you are ready to implement your strategies, you will find the process less stressful and unpredictable because of the careful planning you have done. Ultimately, you are able to solve problems quicker and reach your targets, without too much deviation from your original roadmap.

FOUR APPROACHES TO PLANNING

There isn't a single way to make a plan. You get to decide how elaborate and strategic your plan will be. Of course, the more detailed your plan, the more time it will take to compile it. But, as mentioned above, spending more time on your plan will save you a lot of time during the execution phase. Generally, there are four approaches to planning, which are:

1. Reactive Planning—Focusing on Past Results

Reactive planning holds the assumption that what has happened before will likely happen again. It is, therefore, safer to plan by looking back at past events and information, instead of present events and information.

Example: If you are planning on losing weight, you are more likely to think back on diet and workout strategies that worked the last time you successfully lost weight. A good portion of your plan will be based on these old strategies since they have been proven to bring the desired results.

2. Inactive Planning—Focusing on Present Experiences

Inactive planning looks at what is happening right now and creates strategies accordingly. Past events and information are seen as unreliable because they don't consider the present moment. The assumption is that things are as good as they are going to get, and any new changes in the future will likely bring negative outcomes.

Example: Whenever you are placed in a new environment, like starting a new job, you don't have a blueprint to work from. This may force you to think on your feet and create new strategies based on current information, such as figuring out how to adapt to the new work culture.

3. Preactive Planning—Predicting the Future

Preactive planning involves making strategies with the future in mind. The present moment is seen as constantly evolving; innovations that are modern today will be outdated in a few years. Planning aims to take advantage of the changes you see happening around you.

Example: Investing money in stocks or property requires preactive planning. The enthusiasm around purchasing an asset is based on the presumption that over time, the asset will increase in value.

4. Proactive Planning—Creating the Future

Proactive planning involves creating a vision for an ideal future, then creating a step-by-step process for achieving that vision. Instead of analyzing how things already are, you take the proactive role and create your desired outcomes. Any changes that are predicted for the future are seen as challenges you will need to overcome to make your ideal future a reality.

Example: When starting a new business, you get the opportunity to envision a world with your products or services in it. Instead of imitating existing businesses, your mission is to find gaps in the market that you can capitalize on. Any obstacles you might face along the way are seen as hurdles that your business plan must address.

It is important to note that there are no best or worst approaches to planning. As you can tell, various situations turn out well when a specific approach to planning is used. However, there are times when your approach to planning can be inappropriate.

A good example of this is the real-life story of two explorers, Roald Amundsen and Robert Falcon Scott, who competed against each other to reach the South Pole (Guest, 2019). Both men were around the same age and had a lot of experience leading explorations of different kinds. Even though they were racing, it was assumed that they would arrive at the South Pole at the same time.

However, what made this particular expedition different was the harsh weather conditions that the two men and their teams would be traveling in. To complete their races without being threatened by the extremely cold weather, they would need to create a failure-proof plan.

Both Amundsen and Scott had plans, but in the end, Amundsen's plan provided more protection against the harsh conditions and obstacles they would face. Below are a few examples of how differently Amundsen and Scott planned for the race:

1. Transportation

Amundsen learned through research that dogs perform well under harsh weather conditions. Thus, he spent time with the Inuit people who live in the northern parts of Canada, so he can learn how to dogsled. Scott selected a range of different ponies which are unsuitable for the Antarctic weather and brand-new motor sleds that his team forgot to test. The dogs were able to transport Amundsen and his team to the South Pole and back, but the ponies gave up and Scott and his team had to push the motor sleds themselves.

2. Supplies

Amundsen planned for the worst-case scenarios, like running out of food or equipment breakdown. Even though his team consisted of five people, he packed three tons of supplies. This meant that even if he accidentally lost supplies along the way, he would have had enough to complete his journey. On the other hand, Scott's team consisted of 17 people, yet he only packed a ton worth of supplies. This meant that if he accidentally lost supplies along the way, his team would be left hungry and stranded. For example, Amundsen packed four thermometers and Scott packed one, which unfortunately broke on their journey.

3. Mindset

Amundsen began preparing for the race years in advance. Even though he was an experienced explorer, he decided to overestimate the obstacles his team would face, rather than underestimate them. As part of his preparation, he adopted a rigorous fitness regime, obtained a Master's certificate in sailing, and planned for situations that would test his survival, like having to eat raw dolphin if his food supplies ran out.

Scott's approach was different. Since he was also an experienced explorer, he underestimated the obstacles his team would face. Because he had already survived extreme conditions, journeying to the South Pole didn't seem like it would be any different from what he had experienced in the past. He planned for the best-case scenarios, and this strategy, unfortunately, backfired.

Amundsen's team made it to the South Pole and back to Norway where they lived. On their journey back home, Scott's team hadn't arrived at the South Pole yet. Their frozen bodies were discovered inside a tent, eight months later. Based on this story, there are six fundamental tips for choosing the right approach to planning:

- **Set yourself up to succeed**. Before you get started on your goal, do the necessary research and prepare for various challenges you might face along the way. Doing research and coming up with alternative strategies can reduce as much risk as possible, and prevent delays when you experience unforeseen events.
- **Consider the worst-case scenarios**. While being optimistic is helpful, your plan must also include alternative options when "Plan A" doesn't work. Create "what if" scenarios with different alternatives to handling them.
- **Have a clear direction and sense of purpose**. It isn't enough to plan how you desire to start your goal and leave the rest to luck. Every step along your journey must be carefully outlined so that you can predict your likelihood of success. Having a definitive purpose can also add structure to your plan and set out a clear roadmap.
- **Create systems to hold yourself accountable**. Even though you might be passionate about chasing the goal, passion alone won't protect you from risks. Every so often, you should be

able to review the progress you have made and make adjustments to your plan. Be flexible enough to adapt to changes in your environment, rather than fixed on your initial plan.

- **See mistakes as opportunities to grow**. Failure can be turned into a valuable learning experience if you choose to learn from your mistakes. Whenever you fail, seek an understanding of what caused the problem and how you can prevent it in the future.
- **Take risks, but make sure they are calculated risks**. Strategic risks are those that you can carefully plan for and weigh the pros and cons. Even though the decision remains risky, you can respond to challenges that arise with speed and focus because you were able to predict them.

Even though your goal may not be to hike to the South Pole, you will need to think about your specific approach to planning. For instance, you may have a goal that would benefit more from reactive than proactive planning. Always choose the approach that can reduce as much risk as possible, create a system that holds you accountable, and makes allowances for worst-case scenarios.

PLANNING FOR DIFFERENT ASPECTS OF YOUR LIFE

Think about it: Your daily routine is built on a plan. It may not be the most effective plan—especially if your time is filled with a lot of unnecessary tasks—but it helps you get work done and maintain close relationships.

The moment you decide that you demand more out of your life, planning will become something you do regularly. This is because to get from point A to point B, you need clear directions. If you reflect on the proudest accomplishments in your life, you will notice that you didn't achieve them by accident. You had a plan that you stuck to, which made it easier to manage your time, money, and effort.

Every worthy goal starts as a dream or desire, but to implement the goal, you must have a plan as well! Regardless of the size of the goal, a standard plan will include the following information:

- specific purpose
- timeframe to complete goal
- time-based tasks (i.e., daily, weekly, or monthly)
- audit on resources available (or required) to assist you

- potential obstacles (and what to do in the event of failure)

Bear in mind that this information is the bare minimum required to create a solid plan. The more detailed your plan is, the more risks you can avoid. Nevertheless, even a basic plan is better than not having one at all. Just imagine how difficult it would be to throw a party without having a theme, setting a date, having access to cash, selecting budget-friendly suppliers, or creating a plan B in case the weather conditions change on the day.

It is also worth mentioning that the power of planning can be effective in different aspects of your life, big or small. For example, you have heard about business plans, which are created when aspiring entrepreneurs set out to launch their startups. However, there are also plans to:

- break bad habits/adopt healthier habits
- lose weight/gain muscle
- prepare for a vacation/relocation to a different city
- accumulate wealth/save more money
- find a romantic partner/start a family
- get a promotion at work/prepare for career transition

- reduce stress and anxiety/become a happier person

The great news is that the principles of effective planning don't change depending on your specific goal. This means that after you have successfully achieved a goal in one area of your life, you can utilize the same strategies to plan for a goal in a different area of your life!

EXERCISE: BRAINSTORMING YOUR SUCCESS PLAN

Throughout the book, you will be given plenty of opportunities to practice different planning and goal-setting strategies. This first exercise will help you transfer your ideas on paper and think about some of the major goals you desire to pursue, and what it would take to pursue them.

Answer the following six questions on the line spaces provided.

1. What do you want to do/who do you want to be in your life? (Note: You don't need to include the specific details about your hopes and dreams yet—you will get to clarify your goals in the following chapters).

2. By when would you like to complete your goal? Set a reasonable time frame.

3. What motivates you to pursue this goal? What is the driving force behind your desire?

4. What are you willing to sacrifice to achieve your goal? For example, what habits are you determined to break? How much money are you willing to spend? What different lifestyle choices will you make?

5. Break down the goal into smaller tasks that you can perform on a daily, weekly, monthly, or yearly basis. Note that some tasks may need to be repeated more than once, regularly.

6. Who can you reach out to for support? For example, are there some friends and family you can contact whenever you need someone to hold you accountable? Or do you have a business mentor who can guide you through the early stages of building a startup?

Lastly, combine the answers from 1–6, and create a statement that you can look at regularly, make adjustments to, and memorize.

CHAPTER TAKEAWAYS

Time is a precious commodity because it is something you can't get back. If you desire to see meaningful change in your life, the best time to start planning is NOW. While planning can take a lot of time in and of itself, it can increase your chances of achieving the desired results. It allows you to consider every aspect of your goal, including the worst-case scenarios.

Starting from the next chapter, you will learn various strategies on how to set up a successful plan and eliminate as many risks along the way. The first strategy we will look at is how to clarify your goals and focus on what you want.

2

THE IMPORTANCE OF CLARITY

A lack of clarity could put the brakes on any journey to success.

— STEVE MARABOLI

WHY HAVING CLEAR GOALS IS CRITICAL

A young monk was an apprentice at a monastery. As part of his 12-month training, he was required to take a vow of silence. But there was one exception to the rule. Every four months, the apprentice would be allowed to utter two words only.

After the first four months, the head monk approached the apprentice and asked him what his two words were.

"Floor... cold," said the apprentice.

"Ah, I see," replied the head monk.

Another four months passed, and the head monk went over to check on the apprentice again. Once again, the apprentice was given an opportunity to utter two words.

"Food... disgusting," said the apprentice.

"Ah, I see," replied the head monk.

Finally, the 12-month period was over, and the head monk called the apprentice into his office for a feedback meeting.

"What are your two words, after this 12-month apprenticeship?" asked the head monk.

"I... quit!" exclaimed the apprentice.

If you were asked to summarize your goal in two words, could you do it? There is an old saying that it only takes a few words to tell the truth. I'm not sure how accurate this statement is, but one thing is for sure —when your words are few, the message is clear!

When it comes to creating your success plan, clarity is critical. When you are clear about what you are chasing, you are able to be specific about the action steps to get there. You may also find it easier to rule out tasks or options that won't move you closer to your goal, which speeds up the decision-making process. Clarity about your goals will also prevent what is known as paralysis by analysis; the act of collecting and analyzing information to the extent of doubting yourself, or being afraid to take the first step.

Compare the goals below and notice the difference between them.

- **Goal 1:** I want to get promoted to senior marketing manager.
- **Goal 2:** I want to become the senior marketing manager, reporting to the marketing director. To achieve this goal, I will need to pursue an MBA, which will take between 1–3 years. During that time, I will focus on strengthening relationships with my team, as well as the marketing execs. I will also increase my hours at work by approximately five hours every week (an extra hour per day). After every three months, I will perform a self-evaluation to review my work performance.

The first thing you may have noticed is that both goals are chasing after the same outcome—to become a senior marketing manager. However, the second goal provides greater clarity by including a lot more detail. The additional information gives the goal a sense of direction; you can see clearly what is required to achieve the goal. Therefore, when it comes to being focused and motivated, the second goal will likely produce more successful outcomes.

People who can clearly articulate what they want tend to outperform those who have a vague idea of what they want. Even though there is a time and place for visualizing your goal or creating vision boards, at some point, you will need to define what you want and have an understanding of what it takes to achieve it.

CLARITY BEFORE TAKING ACTION

One of the reasons why my first business failed was that I didn't have clarity on how I was going to fund the business during the startup phase. I thought that having a few thousands of dollars in savings would be sufficient to get the business off the ground. But, in reality, those few thousands of dollars couldn't stretch more than six months.

I was disappointed, to say the least, when I had to go back to the drawing board after spending so much money on products and marketing. Nonetheless, this gave me an opportunity to only refine my business model, but also clarify how I was going to financially keep my business afloat.

This second time around, I created a two-year financial plan, complete with weekly, monthly, and yearly budgets. I considered every possible expense and tried to cut costs as much as possible. On top of accounting for every expense, I created clear revenue goals. Each month, I set a target for how much money I wanted to generate from sales. Even though I didn't always reach those sales targets, having them in place made it easier to manage my time and effort.

After the first year, my business started to break even. This was a positive sign that proved that the business was making enough money to cover its monthly expenses. By the 18-month mark, the business began making profits, and the rest—as they say—is history!

The difference between my first and second attempts at starting my first business was that on the second try, I had more confidence to take calculated risks. What gave me confidence? The ability to clarify my goals and work on specific tasks to achieve them. For instance, my time was no longer spent trying to tick every box that startup businesses are told to tick. Instead, I drew up a few strategic objectives that would guide my decision-making process and help me keep my business running on a lean cash flow.

Gaining clarity before investing any more money was a lifesaver! It meant that I could avoid incurring unnecessary expenses—which would get me into deeper financial trouble. It also meant that I could replace my vague goal with a more well-defined and clearer one. The downside was that I had to start from scratch and refine my business plan. But, the payoff was that I knew exactly what I needed to do to achieve my objectives.

Can you think about a recent goal that you were not able to achieve because of a lack of clarity? Think back to the amount of preparation and planning you carried out before taking action. Would you say that you knew exactly what you wanted, and what it would take to achieve that, before taking action? All of us fall into the trap of thinking that we can go with the flow and learn new information along the way. But, before long, we realize that unless we are clear on what we are doing, why we are doing it, and how we can do it most efficiently, we simply won't have the desire or resources available to accomplish our goals.

There are three steps that you can practice to gain more clarity about your goals. Consider each step below and answer the questions in the line space provided.

Step 1: Focus on WHAT You Want to Achieve

Objective: Answer the "What" of Your Goal

The first step is to define what you want to achieve. It is tempting to just think about the most lavish idea, which may not be practical. But, I would caution you not to do this. At the end of the day, you want to pursue a goal that is realistic and relevant to your life.

For example, winning the lottery might be a dream come true, but what are your odds of actually winning the lottery? According to the Lottery Guru (n.d.), the odds of winning the U.S. lottery jackpot are 1 in 25,989,600 million. Therefore, this goal would not be an appropriate one to strive toward.

Answer the following questions to clearly define *what* you want to achieve.

1. What exactly is your goal?

2. What outcomes are you hoping to get at the end?

3. Is your goal realistic and relevant to your life? Provide evidence.

Step 2: Focus on WHY You Want to Achieve It

Objective: Answer the "Why" of Your Goal

The next step is to explore the motivation behind your goal. In general, the more desirable a goal is, the easier it is to encourage yourself to stay on course until you accomplish it. There is no use in pursuing a goal that doesn't carry any significance to you. For instance, what your friends, spouse, or family members desire for you may not be what you desire for yourself. Yes, you might be driven to make them happy, but soon enough, you will grow tired and resentful of living your life to please others.

When defining your "why," search deep within you and think about why achieving the goal matters so much. When your "why" is clear, believable, and inspiring, you will naturally feel compelled to do whatever it takes to make your dream a reality.

Answer the following questions to clearly define *why* you want to achieve your goal.

1. Why is it important to pursue and achieve your goal?

2. What positive change will occur in your life when you achieve the goal?

3. How will achieving this goal positively impact your relationships?

4. What lifelong dream or passion does this goal address?

Step 3: Focus on HOW You Will Achieve It

Objective: Answer the "How" of Your Goal

The final step is to think about the best method (as well as alternative methods) for pursuing your goal. This step involves outlining the detailed process of getting from where you are to where you desire to be. The commonly used approach is to break down your goal into smaller, manageable tasks that you can perform periodically (i.e., daily, weekly, or monthly). Breaking down your goal in this way allows you to manage your time wisely and adjust your plan whenever you receive positive or negative feedback.

Please note that for most goals, there are several acceptable methods you can use. However, not every method will suit your needs and lifestyle. For example, you might want to complete a university degree, but due to your busy work schedule, don't have time to study full-time. You would need to find a method that caters to your busy lifestyle, such as becoming a part-time student, while helping you complete your degree within the shortest amount of time.

Answer the following questions to clearly define *how* you want to achieve your goal.

1. Working backward, what are the major milestones (at least three) that you will need to reach in order to achieve your goal? Write down each milestone, starting from the final one before you achieve the goal.

2. Milestone 1: Do some research on the first milestone and write down specific tasks that you can commit to, in order to reach the milestone. You can categorize the tasks into daily, weekly, and monthly tasks.

3. Milestone 2: Do some research on the second milestone and write down specific tasks that you can commit to, in order to reach the milestone. You can categorize the tasks into daily, weekly, and monthly tasks.

4. Milestone 3: Do some research on the third milestone and write down specific tasks that you can commit to, in order to reach the milestone. You can categorize the tasks into daily, weekly, and monthly tasks.

5. Reflect on your list of tasks and write down the new behaviors you can practice to keep yourself accountable to your goal and remain committed to your method.

As you complete these three steps, you will notice that your goal becomes more practical. If at first you felt overwhelmed by the process of achieving your goal, you will begin to feel more at ease because the steps you need to take are clearly laid out for you. When you have clarity, you know how to spend your time, which tasks are most important, and how much work you will need to put in. All of this preparation increases your chances of success!

EXERCISE: BE CLEAR ON YOUR WEEKLY SCHEDULE

Many goals will come with weekly commitments. For example, if you are planning on running a marathon, you may need to train weekly, or if you want to heal from heartbreak or trauma, you may need to schedule weekly therapy sessions. It is important to think about how your weekly commitments will fit into your current routine. Consider how each day might look, and how much time you will have to focus on your goal.

Once again, being realistic about your current work and life responsibilities will help you avoid overloading your day with tasks, to the extent of feeling stressed and anxious about your goal. Ideally, when you think about your goal, you don't want to feel forced to make time. It should be a pleasure to shift your focus to your goal and work on tasks you find meaningful.

Therefore, planning your week in advance (on Saturday or Sunday evening) will help you clarify the objectives for each week, which tasks are most urgent to complete, and what "making progress" will look like for various aspects of your life. The plan for your week doesn't need to have a lot of detail, but it should include just enough information to create a structure for each day.

Here are three steps to plan your week.

Step 1: Focus on the Bigger Picture

Focusing on the bigger picture gives you perspective on what you are working toward, and how far along you are to achieving your major goals. Before reviewing your weekly tasks, take a look at your monthly and yearly goals. Make a note of any upcoming monthly goals you will need to spend more time focusing on this week. For example, if you have to submit a quarterly report in two weeks, you might want to invest more of your time working on it.

Step 2: Make a List of Weekly Staples

Your weekly staples are those tasks that don't change from week to week, such as going to work for eight hours, picking up your kids from school, or taking your pet for a walk. Make a list of these weekly staples (or review them if you already have a list). Keep your staples between 3–7 tasks. When you are ready, add your weekly staples to your weekly schedule. Below is a clean schedule (including weekdays only) that you can use.

Time	Mon	Tue	Wed	Thu	Fri
6:00 a.m.					
7:00 a.m.					
8:00 a.m.					
9:00 a.m.					

10:00 a.m.					
11:00 a.m.					
12:00 p.m.					
1:00 p.m.					
2:00 p.m.					
3:00 p.m.					
4:00 p.m.					
5:00 p.m.					
6:00 p.m.					
7:00 p.m.					
8:00 p.m.					

Step 3: Make a List of Goal-Related Tasks

Your goal-related tasks may be part of your weekly staples (i.e., going to the gym if your goal is to lose weight), or they may be tasks that change from week to week (i.e., focusing on different business tasks). Create a list of all the goal-related tasks you desire to focus on this week. When doing this step, avoid thinking about the bigger picture. Focus specifically on how you plan on making progress toward your goal this week.

When you are ready, refer back to your weekly schedule and *find time* for your goal-related tasks. If your schedule is already fully-booked, think of ways to cut back time on certain tasks, or delegate them to someone else. If your schedule allows, you can also group related tasks to save time. Remember, you won't always have free time, but if you are determined, you can find it.

Redesign your weekly schedule with your goal-related tasks included.

Time	Mon	Tue	Wed	Thu	Fri
6:00 a.m.					
7:00 a.m.					
8:00 a.m.					
9:00 a.m.					

10:00 a.m.					
11:00 a.m.					
12:00 p.m.					
1:00 p.m.					
2:00 p.m.					
3:00 p.m.					
4:00 p.m.					
5:00 p.m.					
6:00 p.m.					
7:00 p.m.					
8:00 p.m.					

Note that your priorities for each week can change. This is fine, as long as you are seeing progress (no matter how small it is). There will also be weeks where your focus is on completing tasks that you didn't get to complete the previous week. These are known as catch-up weeks and can be a great time to review your plans and check in with yourself too. Your weekly schedule should be used as a guide, not a strict standard that you need to enforce. For instance, when you are feeling tired and need to take a break, it is okay to postpone a task for later or the following day.

CHAPTER TAKEAWAYS

Vague goals can't positively drive your performance. Without a clear goal, you can get easily distracted or overwhelmed by the different ways you can go about achieving your goal. Since not every method will necessarily work for you and your lifestyle needs, you need to figure out what exactly you want and how you desire to structure your process and spend your time.

Now that you have learned how to clarify your goal, let's move on to the next strategy for creating a successful plan—knowing your big "why."

3

KNOWING YOUR "WHY"

Why did you get out of bed this morning, and why should anyone care?

— SIMON SINEK

WHAT IS A SENSE OF PURPOSE?

Have you ever gone through a season in your life where you were on autopilot? Like an airplane cruising in the sky, you went through the motions of waking up, going to work, driving back home, and going to sleep–in that order? This lifeless routine may have continued for several months or years, until, eventually, you wondered, "What's the point of all of this?"

A life without purpose is a life without meaning. Even though your life may be full of activity and plenty of responsibilities, you don't have a clear focus. On the surface, you might appear to be a responsible adult who is checking every box, yet you can't explain the meaning behind your work, friendships, or daily habits.

A sense of purpose is what makes your ordinary life feel extraordinary. Every decision that you make is informed by a strong desire, vision, or principle that shapes how you live and the goals you strive for. If you have experienced a turbulent life full of many highs and lows, having a sense of purpose can ground you and offer much-needed direction and stability.

Purpose can be defined as the "why" behind everything that you do. It is a deep-seated, and often unconscious, motivation that allows you to be productive, build relationships, pursue your goals, and maintain good health. It is important to note that not having a purpose doesn't mean that you are not influenced by someone else's. As the saying goes, "You are the sum of who you surround yourself with." It is easy to be convinced by another person's way of life, to the extent that you adopt the same values, attitudes, and behaviors.

For example, if you grew up in a family of doctors, it is understandable why you would desire to pursue a career in medicine. Or, if many of your friends prioritize health by staying active, it is understandable why you would too. Therefore, even when you haven't yet discovered your "why," it's possible that you can adopt someone else's "why" and pursue goals that are not aligned with your deepest heart's desires.

Finding your purpose requires a conscious decision to investigate what matters most to you in life. To do this, you may need to increase your self-awareness and be willing to probe into your childhood and past experiences to find clues. The beauty of finding your purpose is that it encourages you to cultivate a more genuine relationship with yourself. Instead of going with the masses and being led by social and environmental trends, you take the time to consider your interests, passions, talents, and ideal lifestyle!

The Relationship Between Purpose and Success

Purpose isn't only necessary when your goal is to discover your hidden talents. Your purpose can also help you live a successful life, no matter how you define success. Think of purpose as the seed that is sown in the soil that later grows to become a tall fruit-bearing tree.

When you find your purpose and rebuild your life accordingly, you may need to rethink certain lifestyle habits, adjust certain goals, or end certain relationships. This process doesn't seem to have any payoff until you start to see the life you envisioned in your mind become a reality.

Your purpose becomes evident in the quality of life you enjoy. For example, no longer will you feel stuck between two choices or feel hopeless about your life circumstances. How come? Even during difficult seasons when your life weighs you down, you always have a sense of where you are going and what you desire your life to look and feel like.

Purpose is linked to success because it is what justifies your actions. Many of the goals that are worthwhile aren't achieved overnight. And besides, they require a lot of hard work and effort to accomplish. Furthermore, during the process of achieving your goals, you will need to make some tradeoffs, like living on a lean budget or selling some of your prized possessions.

Without a clear purpose, the journey to success will feel more punishing than gratifying. You might grow to resent some of the sacrifices you need to make because there isn't a strong inner conviction justifying your actions. However, worst of all, at any slight discomfort or obstacle, you might consider giving up, since there is no big "why" keeping you from walking away.

In the sporting world, the name Michael Jordan is synonymous with success and excellence. Throughout his basketball career, Jordan won five Most Valuable Player Awards and six NBA titles and was even inducted into the Naismith Memorial Basketball Hall of Fame.

All of his achievements came as a result of not giving up when faced with rejection and countless failures. In fact, Jordan credits his success to his ability to try harder every time he makes a mistake. "I know that fear is an obstacle for some people, but for me, it is just an illusion," he said, "Failure always makes me try harder on the next opportunity" (Locke, 2015).

What makes Jordan's relentless spirit that much more impressive is the fact that during high school, he wasn't the best basketball player on the court. At some point, his basketball coach booted him off the team due to his poor performance. The question you should be asking yourself is why a high school kid who wasn't talented at basketball and failed on many occasions, would go on to become a top-performing athlete. What was it about this particular sport that kept him motivated to become a better player?

It all boils down to purpose. Since Michael Jordan was a young boy, he had always dreamed of being a basketball player. Not only that, but after watching the U.S. Olympic basketball team compete against Russia, he announced to his family that he would one day become an Olympic basketball champion (Kirkus, 2012).

This was the awe-inspiring purpose that motivated Jordan to develop his basketball skills and continue to show up for practices. Over time, Jordan was able to improve his performance and outperform every player on his high school basketball team. He was then awarded a full athletic scholarship from the University of North Carolina, then went on to play 15 seasons for two NBA teams.

When you are clear about what you want to do, but most specifically, *why* you want to do it, you are proactive about achieving your goals. This is the major difference between someone with purpose and someone without. The purpose-driven man or woman can shape their life around a vision or strong desire. This allows them to focus on the vision or desire, as though their entire life depended on it! Instead of waiting for things to happen, they create a plan and take meaningful action, until they achieve the desired results.

HOW TO FIND YOUR PURPOSE

Your purpose can be something that excites you, like becoming a legendary athlete. However, even more than making you excited, your purpose will make your life feel meaningful.

When you have found your purpose, your unique personality, ambitions, and past life experiences will start to make sense, and you will understand why you were drawn to certain interests, careers, or people.

If you haven't yet found your purpose, there are three different exercises you can practice to get closer to that "Aha!" moment.

Discover Your Ikigai

Ikigai (pronounced "ee-key-guy") is an ancient Japanese concept that can help you find what matters most in your life. The direct translation of the word is "life's worth," which implies that every human life is significant in its own way. Finding your ikigai requires you to find what gives your life significance. The Western interpretation of the concept breaks down ikigai into four interconnected components: what you love, what the world needs, what you can get paid for, and what you are good at. Let's look at each component in more detail.

1. What You Love

Your ikigai will be something that you enjoy doing. Think of the activities that you can spend hours working on, without feeling tired. Or those activities that put a smile on your face, or make you feel glad that you are alive. When you love something, your thoughts always somehow drift to it. During conversations with others, you are reminded of it and can easily share your opinions about it.

On the line space provided below, write down a list of tasks or experiences that you love.

2. What the World Needs

Your ikigai is also something that can improve the well-being of others. Think of the best ways you know how to make a contribution to your family, community, or country. Ask yourself, "How do I enjoy being of value to others?" The good news is that there are so many ways to positively contribute to the world. Even what you might think is a small task can play an important role in the lives of those around you.

On the line space provided, write down the different ways you enjoy helping others. This could be in the context of your family, neighborhood, or country.

3. What You Can Get Paid For

As much as your ikigai contributes to the well-being of others, it should also add value to your life. Making money from your ikigai is not mandatory, but for many people who desire to make their purpose profitable, it is important to make sure that what you are passionate about is something that can be monetized. How much money you make from it is irrelevant. What matters is that you are able to be compensated for the time and effort you spend cultivating your ikigai.

Refer back to the first component (what you love doing) and select activities that you believe can be monetized. If you can think of other interests that you can get paid for, write them down too.

4. What You Are Good At

Enjoying what you do is crucial, but so is being good at it. The fourth component in finding your ikigai is to look for natural talents or skills that you have mastered over time. Leveraging your talents and skills makes achieving success in life a lot easier. You can work longer hours without feeling the strain because you are gifted, or an expert, in what you do.

On the line space provided, write down a list of things you are naturally good at, or have become an expert in over time.

Take these four components and look for the sweet spot where they all merge seamlessly. In other words, find the few tasks or activities that meet all four components (i.e., you love doing it, the world needs it, you can get paid for it, and you are good at it). These tasks or activities reveal what could potentially be your ikigai—the thing that makes your life feel significant!

Confront Your Fears

Sometimes, the only thing stopping you from finding your purpose is fear. For instance, you might fear making a career transition that doesn't turn out like you expected it would. Or you might fear what others might think about your new lifestyle choices. I like the acronym FEAR, which is often used to describe this strong emotion. Fear is defined as:

- False
- Evidence
- Appearing
- Real

If you examine your life, you may find that many of the past decisions you have made were based on false evidence appearing real. Instead of considering the facts, you may have placed a lot of emphasis on "what if" scenarios. You don't need to feel guilty for doing this because as a society, we have been programmed to expect the worst and hope for the best. The threat of failing at a goal is something that many of us experience, at least once in our lifetimes.

In those moments when your fears appear more real than the facts of the situation, you can pause and challenge those assumptions. Ask yourself if what you are thinking or feeling matches reality, or not. Moreover, look for evidence for and against your fears.

For example, yes, you may have every right to fear making a career transition because moving from one industry to another might lower your standard of living. But on the other hand, making the career transition would improve your emotional well-being because you would get to do what you have always been passionate about.

Think about some of the fears that have been holding you back from discovering your purpose. Write down the fear and present evidence for and against it. Below is an example:

Fear: I am afraid that I don't have enough money to go back to school.

Evidence for: Yes, right now I don't have any money kept in savings.

Evidence against: There are other ways of funding college, such as applying for a student loan, applying for work study aid, getting a part-time job, or asking friends and family for contributions.

Think of three more fears and fill out the spaces below.

Fear:

Evidence for:

Evidence against:

Fear:

Evidence for:

Evidence against:

Fear:

Evidence for:

Evidence against:

Embrace Your Core Values

Another exercise to find your purpose is to explore and embrace your core values. Everything that you do in life is informed by the values you uphold for yourself. These values create a sense of order and predictability in your life. When you live based on your values, your words and actions are congruent. Moreover, the decisions you make always have your best interests at heart, and, thus, can help you achieve your dreams.

Your core values describe what matters most in your life. To embrace your core values, it is important to be clear on what they are. Go through the list below and circle every value that resonates with you.

Acceptance	Peace	Service to others	Security
Determination	Friendship	Ethics	Self-control
Kindness	Adventure	Learning	Balancc
Achievement	Socializing	Leadership	Optimism
Success	Empathy	Passion	Teamwork
Family	Independence	Personal growth	Risk-taking
Health	Honesty	Resilience	Vision
Hard work	Communication	Dependability	Wealth
Power	Wisdom	Creativity	Consistency
Innovation	Challenge	Spirituality	Recognition
Playfulness	Commitment	Love	Simplicity

Group all of the similar values into categories. Create a maximum of five categories. Choose one word within each category to represent what the category is about. Below is an example:

Love	**Success**	**Family**	**Achievement**	**Health**
Acceptance	Hard work	Love	Consistency	Balance
Kindness	Innovation	Dependability	Vision	Spirituality
Playfulness		Peace	Power	Personal growth
Passion			Challenge	

Blank template:

Lastly, add a verb at the beginning of each main value to envision what it would look like if it became a part of your purpose. For example, you might write:

- to show love
- to aim for success
- to embrace family
- to multiply achievement
- to promote health

Write down your phrases below. Feel free to turn the phrases into statements, as well as writing in order of priority.

EXERCISE: CREATE YOUR PURPOSE STATEMENT

A purpose statement, also referred to as a mission statement, is a sentence or paragraph that describes who you are, what you believe and value, and most importantly—your purpose in life.

Creating a purpose statement requires you to think about everything that makes your life unique and feel meaningful. You might reflect on your character traits, talents, skills, past accomplishments, and future aspirations.

The benefit of creating a purpose statement is that it answers the "why" to every goal you set out to achieve. If you ever need a reminder of why you are living a certain way or need to work as hard as you do, you can pull out this document and reflect on the underlying motivation. Your purpose statement can also be used as a roadmap to help you make important career, health, lifestyle, or relationship decisions, and stay on track to achieve your goals.

Before you write down your statement, start by brainstorming ideas on what you might like to add. You can use the answers to the exercises completed above as part of your inspiration, and answer a few more questions below:

1. How would you describe yourself? And who do you desire to become?

2. What kinds of compliments do you receive frequently?

3. How do you want to change the world? What lasting impact do you want to leave behind?

4. What is your reason for waking up each morning?

5. Who are the most important people in your life?

6. What would a lifestyle align with your values and goals look like? Describe it below.

After completing the questions, you will be ready to draft your purpose statement. Below are a few tips when writing a purpose statement:

- Use first-person "I" statements.
- Use positive words like can, instead of can't.
- Write down what you want or expect, not what you don't want.
- Make the statement inspiring enough to drive meaningful action.

Write your purpose statement in the line space provided below.

CHAPTER TAKEAWAYS

Finding your purpose is a journey in and of itself. It involves spending time thinking about who you are and what makes your life feel meaningful. This isn't always easy, especially when you have spent the majority of your life being informed by other people's beliefs, values, and expectations. Nonetheless, it is worthwhile to find your purpose because it can justify the reason why you are passionate about pursuing your goals and give you the courage to make tough sacrifices and change your lifestyle, just so you can achieve them.

Now that you have learned about the importance of finding your purpose, let's move on to the next strategy for creating a successful plan—adjusting your mindset.

4

WHY MINDSET MATTERS

Love challenges, be intrigued by mistakes, enjoy effort, and keep on learning.

— CAROL DWECK

YOU ARE WHAT YOU THINK

There is a famous quote by Henry Ford that says, "Whether you think you can, or think you can't, you're right" (Goodreads, 2019). This quote is often used when explaining the importance of having a good attitude; however, it can also be used when exploring what a mindset is, and why it is so valuable.

Ford discovered that human beings had the power to shape their realities with their thoughts. What a person thinks about themselves, or believes about their life, ends up becoming a self-fulfilling prophecy, something that they unconsciously attract. For example, someone who doubts their ability to succeed may remain stuck in the same cycles and routines because they don't believe they deserve or can achieve better.

Many years ago, I was curious to find out just how powerful my thoughts were in shaping my reality. The first few years of living in Canada were stressful, to say the least, and the only thing I saw around me were problems and more problems! Nothing seemed to work out for me, which made me question whether immigrating to a new country was a good idea.

Feeling hopeless and at the mercy of external circumstances, I decided to reframe my thoughts. Even though my life was full of challenges, I made an effort to see them as opportunities. For every setback, I believed that there was a hidden lesson to be learned. I will be honest, on some occasions, it was tough trying to find the lesson, but because I was determined to, I did!

Over the course of a few months, something remarkable started to happen. For every challenge that I perceived as an opportunity, I was able to find a solution. For example, living on a tight budget encouraged me to plan spending wisely, and not having a vehicle meant that I could walk and take public transit to enjoy the beautiful views of the city.

I was surprised to discover that my thoughts were truly powerful in shaping my reality. How I perceived my life determined whether I would have more positive or negative life outcomes. From that moment onward, I decided to watch my thoughts carefully and be selective about what I chose to believe about myself, my capabilities, and my life.

WHAT IS A MINDSET?

A mindset can be defined as the mental rules that inform how you view and appreciate life. These rules are based on a set of beliefs, values, and attitudes that influence how you perceive yourself, the actions you take, and the way you interact with people.

Your mindset is extremely important because it determines how you perceive reality. For example, imagine that you were holding a glass full of water. The moment you add food coloring into the water, the color changes, and what you see changes too. The water is still water, but you don't see it that way. Similarly, your mindset colors your life.

Oftentimes, the experiences you go through in life are objective. For example, being unemployed is an objective experience, and so is losing a loved one or purchasing a new vehicle. However, your mindset gives these objective experiences personal significance. You might feel humiliated about being unemployed due to feeling like a failure, or you might feel at peace after losing a loved one because you knew how much they suffered while they were alive. Someone else might feel the opposite way about the same events because of the unique personal significance they place on the experiences.

Therefore, you can see that it isn't so much about what happens to you that affects your moods and behaviors, but, instead, how you perceive what is happening to you. Some people can recover from situations that others are still stuck in. Their ability to triumph over adversity boils down to the type of mindset they have.

Some people can succeed against all odds. Even though they started with barely any resources, they found a way to accumulate wealth over time. "How do they do it?" you might ask. It's simple. They have adopted a type of mindset that helps them remain committed to their goals, despite setbacks.

TYPES OF MINDSETS

There are different types of mindsets, which can be classified as either helpful or harmful to your personal development. Each mindset lies on a scale and typically coexists with other related mindsets. In other words, you can display 30% of mindset A, 50% of mindset B, and 20% of mindset C. The good news is that whenever you become dissatisfied with your mindset, you can develop more of the ones you desire! Your brain certainly can reprogram your thinking patterns and help you adopt new beliefs and attitudes.

Below is a list of the different types of mindsets, presented in pairs.

Fixed vs. Growth Mindset

A growth mindset is based on the belief that you can become a better version of yourself. Your starting position in life is not seen as the final position. Throughout your life, as you gain new experiences, you can learn different skills, outgrow certain habits, and achieve your wildest dreams.

A fixed mindset is based on the belief that who you were five years ago, is the same man or woman you are today. You may have deep insecurities that prevent you from believing that you can transform, or that you deserve a shot at success. As a result, you try to avoid change as much as possible, and stick to what has been tried and tested to work.

The main differences between a fixed and growth mindset are:

- A growth mindset accepts that it doesn't know everything. A fixed mindset will convince you that it is right, all of the time.
- A growth mindset seeks to learn from others who are more experienced. A fixed mindset doesn't trust the guidance received from others.
- A growth mindset believes that weaknesses can be improved. A fixed mindset looks at weaknesses as permanent flaws.
- A growth mindset accepts help. A fixed mindset believes they need to do everything on their own.
- A growth mindset believes that failure is a learning opportunity. A fixed mindset believes that failure is a result of incompetence.

Scarcity vs. Abundance Mindset

The concept of a scarcity mindset was initially used to describe how people in poverty-stricken environments viewed life. However, as time went on, people from different socio-economic backgrounds were found to display this type of mindset too. A scarcity mindset is based on the belief that the resources and opportunities offered in life are few and far between.

The assumption is that there will never be enough to go around, and, therefore, you must settle for what you have. The focus is constantly on what is lacking, missing, or taken away from you. A scarcity mindset also affects how you manage your resources. For example, you might feel physically sick or threatened whenever you spend money or postpone pursuing your goals because you believe that you don't have time.

An abundance mindset is based on the belief that life is generous. For example, whenever you are faced with a crisis, you believe that a solution can be found, or when you are single, you don't lose hope in finding true love. This type of mindset is optimistic in nature, but don't confuse it with naivety. For instance, not paying your bills on time will have negative consequences, regardless of how hopeful you are to improve your financial management.

The main differences between a scarcity and abundance mindset are:

- A scarcity mindset believes that it needs to outshine others to succeed. An abundance mindset believes that the success of one is the success of all.

- A scarcity mindset quickly gives up when it is confronted with challenges. An abundance mindset looks for alternative plans and solutions.
- A scarcity mindset is reluctant to spend time, money, and information. An abundance mindset believes in uplifting others in different ways.
- A scarcity mindset believes in the concept of survival of the fittest. An abundance mindset believes in collaboration and a sense of community.
- A scarcity mindset needs control to not feel anxious. An abundance mindset is open and trusts that everything will work out just fine.

Mindful vs. Mindless Mindset

You have probably heard about mindfulness, an Eastern practice that encourages living in the moment. One of the benefits of practicing mindfulness is being able to redirect your focus on what is happening right now. This ends the cycle of overthinking and activates your logical mind. As such, a mindful mindset encourages paying attention to the sensations and activities taking place in this moment.

Doing this can reduce stress and anxiety, as well as increase your alertness.

A mindless mindset occurs when you are unable to ground your thoughts, focus on what is happening right now, or complete a task or activity without getting distracted. Your mind is all over the place, frantically jumping from one thought to the next, without getting any rest. Making logical decisions under this mental state can be tough because your mind cannot hold any thought long enough to examine it.

The main differences between a mindful and mindless mindset are:

- A mindful mindset makes conscious decisions. A mindless mindset makes unconscious decisions.
- A mindful mindset understands the consequences of its actions. A mindless mindset acts impulsively and doesn't consider the consequences.
- A mindful mindset is open and non-judgmental. A mindless mindset is rigid and unconsciously judgmental.
- A mindful mindset asks questions when it doesn't understand something. A mindless mindset makes assumptions.

- A mindful mindset can find the silver lining in difficult situations. A mindless mindset is threatened by difficult situations.

It is possible to adjust your mindset whenever you are ready to experience life from a fresh perspective. This adjustment doesn't happen overnight; however, the more intentional you are about challenging your current beliefs and reframing your thoughts, the easier it will become to shift from one mindset to another.

THE RIGHT MINDSET IN PLANNING

Having the right mindset is essential for planning. This is because a good plan requires a lot of thought, and how can you think clearly when you are not in the right mindset? But besides being in the right frame of mind, planning encourages you to make many decisions about the what, why, and how of your goal. If you are not able to think openly and optimistically about your action steps, you might experience self-doubt while putting together your plan. Some action steps may not seem achievable to you when in reality, you have the capabilities to achieve them.

There are so many instances in my life where I abandoned my plans. It wasn't because I was confused about what I wanted or how I would go about achieving it.

The real reason was that I wasn't in the right frame of mind. My mindset was completely off the mark, and the moment I would experience a setback, I would give up.

You have probably been in the same boat, where you were motivated to pursue a goal or embrace a certain change, and backed out the moment you experienced a challenge. In your head, you thought about a million excuses to justify why you quit, but the truth is that your beliefs and attitudes let you down. If only you had spent some time reprogramming how you think, perhaps your outcomes would have been different. Who knows? The point in all of this, however, is that your planning is futile if it is done with the wrong mindset.

To get yourself in the right mindset to plan, there are a few questions that you can ask:

1. Why Do You Need to Start Planning?

What are some of the goals you desire to accomplish that require a solid plan? How can planning for these goals make the process of achieving them easier? And lastly, how will planning help to integrate your goals into your daily schedule?

Answer these questions in the space provided below:

2. How Will Your Productivity Improve With Planning?

Consider how much time you could save if you had a schedule, the amount of money you would save if you had a budget, or how consistent you would be in your training if you had a fitness plan.

Write down some of the practical ways that having a specific goal-related plan can benefit you.

3. What Are the Potential Obstacles to Your Success?

Part of getting into the right mindset for planning is anticipating future challenges and preparing yourself in advance. Every goal will come with its own set of challenges.

Consider some of the challenges that might come with your particular goal. For each challenge, think of two or three viable solutions.

PREPARING YOUR MIND FOR CHANGE

Change is an inevitable part of life, even though many times we are not ready to embrace it. For several reasons, we can perceive change as threatening. For example, the idea of changing jobs can be frightening regardless of how necessary the transition may be. Or, for someone who desires to improve their physical health, going on a weight-loss journey can sound daunting despite the positive benefits it may come with.

There is no easy way to accept change, especially for those of us who find safety in our comfort zone. Nonetheless, we can prepare ourselves in advance for upcoming changes in our lives to make the transition as smooth as possible. A preparation stage is useful because it allows us to do our research, weigh the pros and cons of our decisions, seek feedback from others, and get ourselves in the right frame of mind. By the time we are ready to take action, we have already mentally prepared ourselves for the highs and lows of the journey ahead.

There is a concept in sports psychology known as mental rehearsal. Before the day of a competition, an athlete visualizes the outcomes of the match and how well they will perform. Famous top-performing athletes like Muhammad Ali and Michael Phelps were known to do this as part of their preparation for big matches. Being able to see their victories before entering the boxing ring or swimming pool helped these two legendary sportsmen get into the right mindset.

Preparing your mind for change requires you to understand the five logical levels of change. This idea is borrowed from neurolinguistic programming (NLP) and is based on a simple model for looking at any new situation. The five logical levels are (Bundrant, 2019):

- identity
- beliefs
- capabilities
- behaviors
- environment

Identity refers to who you are and the different roles you play in your life. When you are about to embark on change, you may need to consider how the change will affect who you are as an individual, as well as a parent, friend, spouse, or coworker. Be prepared to be motivated by different goals, to outgrow certain habits or relationships, or mature in character.

Change will also modify your beliefs. Perhaps for the last 5–10 years, you have been accustomed to looking at life from a certain perspective. However, now that you are ready to embrace new experiences, you are encouraged to be more open-minded and absorb new knowledge. Be prepared for your core values to change, as they reflect the new standards you wish to uphold. For example, you may have valued wealth creation for the past decade, but now that you are embarking on a new journey, you value mental and physical well-being instead.

Capabilities refer to your skillset and the way you choose to do things. Change often triggers growth, which means that in order to embrace the new way of life, you may need to acquire a new set of skills or adopt new strategies. For example, if you are about to go on a journey of personal development, you will need to learn cognitive and self-regulation skills to help you process past trauma and connect to yourself on a deeper level.

Another aspect of your life that will likely change as you shift from one season to the next is your behavior. Each season of your life demands different behaviors. Just imagine how inappropriate it would be for a middle-aged person to display typical adolescent behaviors, or for an entrepreneur to behave like someone who reports to a boss. Fortunately, changing your behaviors isn't something that requires a lot of conscious effort. You will notice that you automatically act differently when your identity and beliefs change. Your job is to reinforce the new behaviors so that they become positive habits.

Lastly, part of preparing for change means being comfortable changing your environment. Environment refers to the places and people with whom you spend most of your time. Some environments don't accommodate the type of change you desire, and others that support it. For example, hanging around people who drink alcohol excessively can be overwhelming for someone who desires a sober life. Or, working in a highly stressful workplace can be challenging for someone who desires a more harmonious work-life balance.

By working through these five logical levels of change, you can prepare yourself for what you may be exposed to on your journey. It can also allow you to plan for worst-case scenarios, so you can feel confident in unfamiliar life situations.

CONTINUOUS LEARNING IS THE KEY TO SUCCESS

Continuous learning is the ability to remain curious on an ongoing basis. Your mind is constantly looking to absorb new skills and knowledge, or learn from trusted experts and mentors. This type of approach to learning is not something that you are born with. Over time, and consistent practice, you learn to become a continuous learner. In general, if you identify as having a growth or abundance mindset, you are likely displaying this type of approach whenever taking on new challenges.

There are some benefits of having an open and curious mind toward learning, which include:

- Being able to improve your performance or competence at work, or while working on your personal goals.
- Having the ability to network and build meaningful relationships with people from different social, cultural, and economic backgrounds.
- Displaying confidence in the face of adversity, due to the vast amount of knowledge you have obtained that can assist you in finding the right solutions.
- Enriching your private life with meaningful hobbies and passions that stimulate your mind or allow you to tap into your creative mind.
- Staying up-to-date with the latest social, political, or economic changes that impact your welfare, and being ready to take action when a crisis hits.

Continuous learning doesn't look the same for everyone. There are generally three ways that you can engage in continuous learning.

Formal Learning

Formal learning is the pursuit of skills and knowledge through traditional institutions, like colleges, training institutions, or universities. The type of information you are exposed to has been pre-determined and structured to meet specific learning outcomes. Examples of formal learning tools include:

- college or university degree, diploma, or certificate
- training programs driven at work
- external training workshops and conferences
- online courses from e-learning platforms or formal institutions

Social Learning

Social learning is less structured and more experiential. It involves learning from discussions you have with friends and family, mentors and coaches, or watching an insightful video. The aim here is to gain knowledge by learning from other people's lived experiences. While this knowledge may not always be factual, it can allow you to see things from a different perspective. Examples of social learning tools include:

- discussions on forums, blogs, or social media
- taking advice from a trusted friend or family member
- collaborating with coworkers
- on-the-job training

Self-Directed Learning

Self-directed learning involves doing your own research to gain new insights and knowledge. Here, you don't rely on a structured course or mentor to share knowledge, but rather, your own summary notes and well-written plans. Examples of self-directed learning tools include:

- teaching yourself therapeutic techniques
- reading a skills-based book
- watching an instructional video
- experimenting with different strategies and finding those that work for you

On a day-to-day basis, you can engage in continuous learning by showing curiosity in your personal and professional life. Don't fall into the trap of believing that you know it all; that type of belief reflects a fixed mindset, which is the antithesis of continuous learning. Below are a few suggestions on ways that you can display curiosity in everyday situations:

- Have a book that you are reading. If possible, explore genres that are outside of your comfort zone.
- When you don't understand a word or figure of speech, Google the meaning or ask for an

explanation.

- On weekends, spend time in different social settings, such as going to a farmer's market on one occasion, then visiting a museum on another occasion.
- Subscribe to different news publications and get the latest updates on world events.
- Expand your professional network by attending various corporate events, mixers, and workshops.

Finally, continuous learning can also be used as a strategy to structure your goals. For example, if you desire to invest in real estate, you can learn more about the world of real estate investing, various investment strategies, and general advice from seasoned investors. All of the knowledge that you acquire about real estate investing can help you create a low-risk investment plan. Continuous learning can offer you a competitive advantage when pursuing your goals, especially when entering industries that you are unfamiliar with.

EXERCISE: CULTIVATE A GROWTH MINDSET

A growth mindset is by far the most useful way of thinking when you desire to implement change. It can help you embrace challenges, improve your performance, reduce stress and anxiety, and maintain an optimistic attitude. Fortunately, this type of mindset can be developed over time. Below are five tips that can help you cultivate a growth mindset:

1. **Play mentally stimulating games**. Complete a crossword puzzle, play Sudoku, or practice your chess skills. Mental games create a fun way to step outside of your comfort zone and embrace challenges.
2. **Switch up your routine**. Take a different route to work, spend your weekend at a different social spot, or go to bed an hour earlier. Doing things in a different order can gently take you off autopilot and help you become more present.
3. **Complete a 30-day challenge**. If you are looking for a fun way to adopt new habits or skills, look for a 30-day challenge. Give yourself 30 days to practice an activity or behavior consistently and track your progress.
4. **Follow an inspirational coach or leader**. Find somebody at work or on social media who you admire. Schedule a meeting with them to ask questions about their daily routine, beliefs, or valuable life lessons. If you cannot meet with

them, purchase a book or course that they have written and treat it as study material.

5. **Ask for feedback**. A great way to adopt a new perspective on your life is to ask for feedback. Approach people whom you trust and ask them to share tips on how you can improve your career, health, or relationships. Reflect on the feedback with an open and curious mind.

CHAPTER TAKEAWAYS

Your mindset is the unique meaning you ascribe to objective experiences. This meaning is determined by your set of beliefs, values, and attitudes about life. By adjusting your mindset, you can change how you see the world and others. However, most importantly, you can be open to the process of outgrowing your current habits, routines, and behaviors and embracing positive change.

Now that you have learned about the importance of adopting the right mindset, let's move on to the next strategy for creating a successful plan—practicing goal setting.

5

THE POWER OF GOAL SETTING

If you don't know where you are going, you will probably end up somewhere else.

— LAWRENCE J. PETER

WHAT IS GOAL SETTING?

So far in the book, we have spoken a lot about goals, specifically the importance of planning around your goals. However, what we haven't yet discussed is the method for creating meaningful goals in the first place. Yes, of course, having a "what," "why," and "how" is important, but is that all it takes? Certainly not.

Setting an achievable goal is a skill. Not only do you need clarity on what you want, but metrics to measure progress and a reasonable time frame to create a manageable schedule. Goal setting sets you up to succeed because it forces you to think about every small detail involved in the process of pursuing your goal. It also creates an adjustable system that clearly shows you what to do, when to do it, and the best methods or tools to use. When you have completed the process of goal setting properly, you won't have to worry about how you will get from point A to point B. Every step is outlined for you!

Goal setting works—but only if you work it! There are five principles to remember whenever you set achievable goals. These include:

1. Commitment—Be Attached to the Goal

How much do you desire to accomplish the goal? This question is extremely important to answer before and during goal setting. There is no hiding the fact you will experience obstacles along the way, which can create physical constraints or leave you feeling demotivated. The higher your commitment, the more likely you are to withstand the pressure, reroute if you have to, but continue moving forward regardless.

2. Clarity—Be Specific About What You Want

We have spoken about the importance of clarity in Chapter 2. The one point that can be emphasized again here, is the value of clarity in establishing a sense of direction. Your chances of achieving your goal are increased when you are clear about where you are heading, and what you can expect along the journey. This allows you to make the necessary preparations and reduce as much risk as possible.

3. Challenge—Pay Attention to the Degree of Difficulty

It is wonderful to set big goals that stretch your mind and encourage you to make positive lifestyle changes. However, be careful not to set goals that are too difficult to achieve. To determine whether a goal is too difficult or not, ask yourself whether it is realistic. For example, does it take into consideration your strengths and weaknesses? Or the limited amount of resources you have available?

4. Complexity—Pay Attention to How Much the Goal Demands

Once again, complex tasks can be a great learning curve. But when tasks are too complex, they can slow down your progress or make the process of achieving your goal feel overwhelming. When determining whether or not a goal is too complex or not, ask yourself how much time and effort it demands from you. Generally, your goal shouldn't steal a lot of time from your work or family. You should be able to integrate it into your existing schedule, without experiencing too much pressure.

5. Feedback—Create a System of Accountability

To judge the effectiveness of your goal-setting efforts, you must be able to create a system of accountability. This might be as simple as reviewing your progress once a week to check if you are still on the right track. Getting feedback on your performance allows you to adjust your plan before exposing yourself to a lot of risks. Positive feedback reveals what you are doing right, and should continue to do more of, while negative feedback reveals what you should replace or adjust.

Helpful Skills to Enhance Goal Setting

There are some skills that can assist you in creating inspiring goals, and hold you accountable to the tasks that you set out to accomplish. If you struggle to maintain motivation or remain consistent during the pursuit, you may be lacking one of the vital skills below:

1. Planning

Goals cannot be achieved spontaneously. You must have a quality plan and good organizational skills to meet all of your objectives and achieve the goal. A solid plan can also be a great time management tool, helping you stay focused on each actionable step and reach your goal within the set time frame.

2. Time Management

As mentioned earlier in the book, time is a precious commodity. Knowing how to spend and save time will help you balance both your daily tasks and your goal-related tasks. Time management will also give you the necessary push to remain consistent in practicing new behaviors so that you can meet your deadlines before losing momentum.

3. Self-Motivation

Your goals reflect your heart's desires. This makes them deeply personal. Nobody else will feel as passionate as you about what you hope to achieve. Self-motivation is what allows you to keep going when friends are few or circumstances don't look promising. The ability to encourage yourself is powerful because it means that you don't rely on external factors to keep you motivated.

4. Flexibility

Ideally, you want plan A to work seamlessly. However, when uncontrollable factors interrupt your plan, you may need to adjust your strategies accordingly. Being flexible allows you to adapt to changing circumstances, without getting derailed, discouraged, or losing momentum.

Flexibility isn't the same as "going with the flow." When you have a flexible approach to your goal, you plan for unforeseen events, creating alternative strategies that you can implement during emergencies. Going with the flow, on the other hand, doesn't encourage planning. It advocates for living in the moment and thinking of solutions on the spot.

5. Self-Regulation

Lastly, along the journey to achieving your goal, you will need to learn how to manage your emotions. It isn't your victories that will trigger strong emotions, but your failures and disappointments. Developing emotional intelligence is an important part of self-regulation. It enables you to understand and express your emotions in positive ways, so you can behave appropriately when overcome with challenges.

SMART GOAL-SETTING TECHNIQUE

Have you ever written down a goal and felt so convicted that you were going to achieve it, but after a few weeks or months of inconsistent attempts, you gave in? Or maybe you were on track to completing a goal, but since you didn't have the right parameters to monitor and measure your progress, you lost momentum?

The toughest part when setting a goal is knowing just how detailed and instructional to make your goal. You might struggle to clearly outline the step-by-step process from getting where you are to where you want to be. Without using the proper goal-setting technique, your goal may come out too general, overly ambitious, or impersonal. To address these issues and ensure that you are creating achievable goals, you can use the SMART goal-setting technique.

The technique, written as an acronym, was created by George T. Doran, a former Director of Corporate Planning for the Washington Water Power Company (Haughey, 2014). The technique was published in an article he wrote in 1981. The aim was to teach managers how to write meaningful objectives. In just five steps, Doran believed that managers could set goals that improved their chances of success.

Below is a breakdown of the SMART goal-setting technique, and questions to help you rewrite your goals.

Specific: Target an Area of Improvement

The first step is to be specific about what you are attempting to achieve. The aim is to provide the big picture idea that can drive your action. Your statement should be able to answer the four "W" questions: what, who, when, and where.

1. What are you trying to accomplish? Be specific about your aim.

2. Who needs to be involved to achieve your goal?

3. When do you expect to complete the goal?

4. Where will you need to visit to achieve your goal?

Measurable: Suggest an Indicator of Progress

The second step is to find ways of quantifying your progress. Think about the different metrics you can use to track your progress. For example, if you are growing your small business, you can quantify progress by the number of new customers that purchase goods. Or, if you are training for a marathon, you can quantity progress by the number of miles you can run without stopping. If you are working on a long-term goal, you can create milestones that indicate when you have reached a significant mark on your journey.

The questions below will help you think about ways to measure your progress:

1. What are the best metrics to measure your performance? For example, is it a specific number, percentage, or ratio?

2. How often will you review progress? For example, will you check in once a day, week, or month?

3. What are key milestones that you can set for your goal?

Attainable: Specify the Tools You Will Use

There are several resources that you need to achieve your goal. Without these resources, progress will be halted. It is important to check before you get started whether you have everything you need to reach your goal. For example, if your goal requires startup capital of $10,000, do you have access to those funds right now? Or, have you at least been pre-approved for a loan?

Below are a few questions to help you determine if your goal is attainable:

1. Do you have the necessary tools or materials to achieve your goal? If not, what arrangements can you make?

2. What skills or knowledge will you need access to?

3.What habits or attitudes will you need to adopt or replace to reach your goal?

Realistic: Reflect on Your Capacity to Achieve Results

The fourth step is to check whether your goal is realistic. In general, if your goal is attainable, then you can conclude that it is realistic. This is because you have already proven that you have what it takes to accomplish your goal. Another way to check if your goal is realistic is to consider if it has been done before. For example, switching to a vegan lifestyle is realistic because there is a whole community of people who have done it before.

Below are a few questions to help you determine if your goal is realistic:

1. Can you *actually* achieve your goal with the resources available to you?

2. Have other people achieved a similar goal? Can you give a testimony of someone that you know who has?

3. Do you have the right mindset to achieve your goal? Provide evidence.

4. List a few personal strengths that can increase your chances of success.

Time-Bound: Suggest a Timeline to Meet Your Goal

The final step is to set a reasonable time frame to reach your goal. Note that you can adjust the time frame if you need more or less time; however, having a set deadline will give you a workable framework to carry out goal-related tasks. Beware of time frames that are too long. It is harder to hold yourself accountable to your goal when you have over a decade to fulfill a goal. But equally so, time frames that are too short can be counterproductive. As a general rule, you can give yourself 9–12 months to complete a goal, then adjust the time frame when necessary.

Below are a few questions to help you determine a reasonable time frame:

1. How far along do you expect to be after 12 months of pursuing your goal?

2. What are the smaller tasks you can complete daily to work toward your goal?

3. What are medium tasks that you can complete on a weekly or monthly basis to work toward your goals?

4. Out of the tasks mentioned above, which are the value tasks that offer the most rewards/bring the most results? How often do you need to practice these tasks?

After reviewing the five steps to creating SMART goals, you are now ready to write down your detailed goal statement. Combine the answers to all of the questions and present the full picture of what you hope to achieve and all the relevant information.

FIVE MENTAL STAGES ON THE JOURNEY TOWARD YOUR GOAL

In the previous chapter, we discussed the importance of having the right mindset when planning for your goal. However, the right mindset will also be instrumental as soon as you begin working on your goal. In fact, the focus and optimism that you display along your journey will be the multiplier of your success!

Maintaining the right mindset can be a breeze when working on short-term goals. For instance, you don't need to show as much patience during the process of achieving your goal because it requires less time. Although, the longer it takes to accomplish the goal, the more complex the goal tends to be, and the more mental focus and commitment you will need to display.

To prepare you for the different hurdles you will face on your journey, it is important to understand the five mental stages you are likely to experience. Some mental stages will make you feel like you are on top of the world, while others will cause you to doubt your ability to succeed. The aim is to notice which mental stage you are in and find healthy coping strategies to reduce stress, increase emotional resilience, and continue to press ahead.

Below are the five mental stages that occur during the pursuit of your goal:

Stage 1: Unjustified Optimism

During the first few weeks and months of chasing your goal, you will experience unjustified optimism. This means that you will display enthusiasm due to the sheer excitement of working on something new. Since it is still early, and you haven't yet seen positive results, you are optimistic for the sake of it, not because you have made progress.

Stage 2: Justified Pessimism

By the time you reach the second stage, you have had a few sleepless nights trying to solve goal-related challenges. The natural enthusiasm that you felt during the early days has waned, and new doubts have crept into your mind. Your outlook on reaching your goal is more balanced: On the one hand, you still believe that you have what it takes to accomplish the goal, but you are not naive about the risks involved, or the sacrifices you may have to make along the way.

Stage 3: Rock Bottom

Not everybody reaches rock bottom on their journey. It all depends on the complexity of the goal, the access to resources, your state of mind, and the types of challenges you are faced with. Signs that you have reached rock bottom are feeling hopeless, being close to the point of giving up, and watching your performance reach an all-time low. You may even notice bad habits developing, such as procrastinating, skipping training, or engaging in mind-numbing activities like drinking or gambling.

When you reach this stage, it is vital to do some introspection. Figure out what factors are contributing to your stress. Is it the scarcity of resources? Lack of support from friends and family? Unforeseen personal issues? Or mental and physical exhaustion? The sooner you can identify what is making you feel tired, stressed, and discouraged, the sooner you can seek help.

Stage 4: Justified Optimism

If you can withstand the discomfort of rock bottom and find a way to climb out of it, you will reach the fourth stage, which is justified optimism. At the beginning of your journey, you were enthusiastic because of the promise of getting ahead. But now, you are enthusiastic because you have overcome many setbacks and have gotten back on track to achieving your goal. You have the same passion as you did before, but now it comes with wisdom!

Stage 5: Fulfillment

Eventually, you will achieve your goal and all of the highs and lows you encountered along the way will be worth it. Having accomplished one of your heart's desires will feel incredible. Not only are you proud of being in a better position now than when you started, but you have a greater appreciation for your life and all of the people who supported you on the journey.

Understanding the various ways that your mind will be tested can help you prepare for each stage. Remind yourself that each stage leads up to the final stage—

fulfillment—which is something you can look forward to!

HOW TO MANAGE MULTIPLE GOALS

Life can place a lot of demands on you, which forces you to pursue multiple goals at the same time. For example, you might be starting a new business, saving up for a mortgage bond with your spouse, and studying part-time—all within the same period!

So, what do you do? Do you select one and forget about the rest? Certainly not. It is possible to manage multiple goals, although it does require double as much focus, commitment, and time-management skills.

Below are three useful strategies that can assist in managing multiple goals:

1. Find the Right Pace

Managing multiple goals doesn't mean working on every goal, each day. On most days, it will be impossible to focus on your daily tasks and find time to work on more than one goal. Therefore, get rid of the expectation that you *must* make progress on every goal, every day of the week.

Look at the timeline for each goal and figure out how much time to invest each week. Some goals won't be as demanding or as complex as others, which means you can spend less time working on them during the week. It doesn't mean that they are less important. It just means that they require less investment.

2. Look for Logical Overlaps

When seeking to work on two or more goals simultaneously, look for logical overlaps. For example, if you have two goals that require research, you can sit at the computer and work on both of them. Or, if you have two career-related goals, you can focus on both of them during the same time slot. Please note that conflicting goals won't have logical overlaps, thus working on them at the same time can be a distraction.

3. Break Down Goals Into Smaller Tasks

Think of your goals as being a series of small tasks, rather than a few big milestones that you work toward. Write down each goal on paper and work backward, listing the tasks that you need to complete to achieve it. For example, if your goal is to purchase a home in the next two years, your list would look like this:

- Make an offer to purchase the home.
- Arrange a home inspection.
- Find your ideal home.
- Hire a real estate agent.

- Get pre-approved for a mortgage loan.
- Assess your credit profile.
- Determine the property you can afford.

Now that your goal has been broken down into smaller tasks, you will be able to schedule each task into your calendar, until you have checked all of them off your list. Do this for every goal that you are working on.

4. Eliminate Distractions

It is hard enough working on a single goal, but when you are pursuing more than one, your time is incredibly valuable. The fewer interruptions you have while completing each task, the more efficiently you will work. Distractions come in all shapes and sizes; from receiving a notification on your phone to getting sidetracked by negative self-talk. When you notice that your mind has wandered off, stop whatever you are doing and take three deep breaths. Allow your breath to gently bring your attention to the current task. Make a note of what the distraction was so that you can be aware when it comes again.

5. Avoid Strict Schedules

Telling yourself that you MUST work on your business plan at 10 p.m. is not a healthy form of encouragement. Avoid rigid schedules that put pressure on you to complete 100% of your tasks each day. Remember, you are human, and as much as you would like to make progress in different aspects of your life simultaneously, your mind and body need a break. Keep your schedule flexible enough to allow for adjustments to plans.

EXERCISE: BREAKING DOWN YOUR GOALS

On the surface, big goals seem daunting! However, when you break them down into smaller actionable steps, you can focus on one task at a time, until you finally reach the goal.

Below is a basic template that you can use to break down your goals and schedule each task into your calendar (an example has been completed for you).

Goal: Finding a new job		
Goal Task	**Time Required**	**Schedule**
Create a career roadmap and goals I would like to accomplish.	2 hours	Saturday morning
Update my résumé with recent skills, work experience, and certificates obtained.	1 hour	Wednesday, after gym.
Browse through job search engines and look for vacancies.	45 minutes	Sunday afternoon

Goal:		
Goal Task	**Time Required**	**Schedule**

Goal:		
Goal Task	**Time Required**	**Schedule**

CHAPTER TAKEAWAYS

Goal setting is an important process during the planning stage of your goal. It offers you an opportunity to think about both small and large steps you will need to take to achieve your goal. To enhance the goal-setting process, ensure that your goals are properly structured so that they are specific, measurable, attainable, realistic, and time-bound. Use the information compiled as a detailed roadmap to determine which action steps to take on a daily, weekly, or monthly basis, respond to unexpected challenges promptly, and adjust your mindset at different stages of your journey.

Now that you have learned about the importance of goal setting, let's move on to the next strategy for creating a successful plan—executing your plan.

6

HOW TO EXECUTE YOUR PLAN

Any goal can be achieved if a strategy is properly executed.

— NITIN NAMDEO

5,127 PROTOTYPES LATER

In 1978, inventor James Dyson noticed that vacuum cleaners with bags lost suction power, as soon as they filled with dust. He came up with a brilliant idea to create a bagless vacuum cleaner using cyclone technology.

The journey between coming up with the idea and testing his designs would take 15 years. In total, Dyson created 5,127 prototypes of his bagless vacuum cleaner, before settling on what he believed was a stellar design. But even after finalizing the design, he still needed to pitch the product to big vacuum manufacturers, so they could license the idea.

To his surprise, none of the leading vacuum manufacturers were interested in licensing the product. It wasn't because the innovation wasn't groundbreaking, but that it would take existing vacuum brands out of business. Many of the brands at the time were making huge profits from the bag and filter technology.

Being rejected by major companies caused Dyson to go a different route. Instead of relying on the sponsorship and support of other corporations, he traveled to different parts of the world and pitched his technology to smaller manufacturing companies.

Eventually, he got a licensing deal with a company based in Japan, and the profits made from that partnership were enough to help him establish the Dyson company in 1993, a company worth multi-billions of dollars today. Dyson also went on to invent several more vacuums, and other hair and home products, like cordless vacuums, hair dryers, and hair straighteners.

THE FOUR STAGES OF SUCCESS

Dyson's success story follows a similar pattern that occurs whenever you undertake a goal. While every success story looks different, there are generally four stages that you will go through before finally accomplishing your goal. There is no set time frame for each stage, since you may be presented with a multitude of obstacles that delay your progress. Nonetheless, knowing which stage you are currently in can be reassuring, and help you focus on what you need to do next.

Below are the four stages of success.

Stage 1: Be Inspired by an Idea

Every worthwhile goal begins with an idea. You are motivated to make a difference in your life, or the lives of others, as a result of an inner desire or an external need that you have identified. At this stage, you aren't required to take action. All that is necessary to do is refine your idea by brainstorming, conducting research, and looking at what other people have done in the past. The ability to tap into your imagination is a multiplier to your success and will naturally lead you to the second stage.

Stage 2: Feel Intrinsically Motivated

The difference between an idea that remains on paper and one that encourages you to take action is the amount of drive behind them. For instance, some ideas sound exciting, but when you think about all of the obstacles you may encounter along the journey, you end up deciding they aren't worth the hassle. On the other hand, some ideas carry so much significance to the extent that you are willing to make all of the sacrifices necessary to bring them to life!

When you are intrinsically motivated, the thought of encountering challenges won't stop you from taking action. You will reach a point where you desire to test your idea or implement your plan. This will naturally lead you to the third stage.

Stage 3: Execute the Idea

The execution stage is where you will carry out the detailed plan that you have spent months preparing. If you have taken the time to structure your goals, you will have clear instructions on how to spend your time on a daily, weekly, or monthly basis. As structured and thorough as your plan might be, note that you can experience delays due to uncontrollable factors or personal issues. Thus, the execution stage is usually the one that takes up most of your time. If you are patient, flexible, and resilient enough, your hard work will pay off, and this will naturally lead you to the fourth stage.

Stage 4: Achieve the Desired Outcomes

After countless hours of work, and overcoming many challenges, you will eventually achieve the desired outcomes. What was once an idea on paper will become a real-life experience and a symbol of success. After you have achieved the desired outcomes, you can decide whether that is where you wish to stop, or not. If you decide to work toward the next level of success, you will need to return to stage one—being inspired by an idea—and repeat the process.

STRATEGIC PLANNING MADE SIMPLE

Strategic planning is a method used by organizations to develop plans and achieve long-term goals. The three steps of strategic planning create a framework that allows teams to create and execute strategic objectives and receive feedback from actions taken.

The good news is that the strategic planning framework is effective outside of the office. Whether your goal is to grow a business, learn a new skill, or outgrow a specific habit, you can use the framework to meet strategic objectives and hold yourself accountable.

Below are the three simple steps that you can practice to create your strategic planning framework:

Determine Your Strategic Position

The first step sets the tone and creates clear expectations for the work you will carry out going forward. As we have mentioned many times throughout the book, it is important to know what you want. A strategic position is a mission or vision statement that explains the purpose of your plan (i.e., what you want to achieve) and paints a picture of what success will look like for you.

Answer the following questions to determine your strategic position, as related to your goal.

1. What problem have you identified? How do you plan on responding to this problem?

2. Who can benefit from your solution?

3. What challenges have you identified that can prevent you from solving this problem? How do you plan on overcoming these challenges?

4. What core values are being met by solving this problem? Explain how.

5. What makes your current solution different from previous attempts?

Combine the answers from the five questions above and create a well-defined strategic position below:

Clarify Your Objectives

Now that you have created a strategic position, you can start to think about smaller objectives that will help you achieve that vision. Your objectives should be practical, meaning you must be able to carry them out using the resources available to you. As time goes on, you can measure your progress by your ability to meet your objectives.

Answer the following questions to clarify your objectives.

1. What role do you play on this journey toward achieving your goal? Write down specific duties and responsibilities that you are in charge of.

2. What tasks need to be completed before a specified date? Write down the list of tasks you need to complete, and the deadline for each.

3. What are some of the behavioral expectations you have for yourself? What kinds of habits might help you maintain those expectations?

4. To improve your performance and achieve better results, what actions do you need to take?

5. What skills or knowledge do you need to learn to improve your chances of success? Write down ideas on how you can acquire these skills or knowledge.

Execute and Review Your Objectives

After setting your objectives, you are ready to take action. Schedule regular review sessions where you can look back at your objectives and assess if you are on track. Sometimes, reviewing progress may lead to revisions. For instance, you might realize that one of your objectives isn't targeted enough and needs to be adjusted. Revisions are also common when your priorities change (this might also trigger changes in your strategic position).

Use the table below to review and revise your objectives. Rate your performance based on the following rating system:

- Much more than expected = 5
- More than expected = 4
- Expected outcome = 3
- Less than expected = 2
- Much less than expected = 1

Date	Objective	Rating	Comments

The strategic planning process is not a once-off thing. As you encounter unique opportunities and challenges, your strategic position and objectives will change. This means that you will need to go back to the drawing board and refine your strategy so that you can achieve optimal results!

FIVE BARRIERS THAT HINDER YOUR PROGRESS

Author of *Alphabet Success,* Tim Fargo, once said, “Opportunity doesn’t make appointments, you have to be ready when it arrives” (Goodreads, n.d.). The purpose of making preparations before executing your plan is to position yourself for opportunity and avoid as many hurdles as possible on your journey.

However, there are times when your plan isn’t to blame for the lack of progress. Instead, what feels like being “stuck” is due to the mental and emotional barriers that get in your way. An unpopular explanation as to why some people fail at achieving their goals is that they sabotage their own plans. When everything seems to be going smoothly, they make choices that favor the “old life,” rather than embracing the “new life.”

Below are five common barriers that can delay or bring your plans to a screeching halt.

1. You Return to the Comfort Zone

Returning to the comfort zone means going back to past beliefs, attitudes, and routines. The temptation to go back often arises when you are confronted with challenges that seek to destabilize you. For example, running out of money while growing a startup business can be stressful.

To deal with the stress, you might turn to past unhealthy coping strategies, like being pessimistic or quitting. The comfort zone may feel familiar, but it cannot bring the kind of growth you are looking for. You must be willing to be uncomfortable for some time, so you can outgrow unproductive behaviors and become a great problem-solver.

2. You Doubt Your Ability to Succeed

Self-doubt is another barrier that can get in the way of executing your plans. We can define self-doubt as the feeling of being uncertain about certain aspects of who you are, such as your competence to achieve a goal. In most cases, self-doubt won't cause you to give up, but it will cause you to do things with half-hearted measures. This is what often slows down your progress.

Overcoming self-doubt requires you to be comfortable with uncertainty. Despite the immense preparation you can invest in your plan, you will never have 100% guarantee that everything you have written down will turn out according to your wishes. Acknowledge the fact that you are a beginner and there are many things you haven't yet learned about life or the process of achieving your goal. Allow yourself to fail enthusiastically, and learn from every setback.

3. You Make Excuses When Things Don't Work Out

You can learn from failure, but it is impossible to learn from an excuse. Whenever things don't work out according to plan, you can collect feedback and find out what went wrong and how you can correct the mistake next time. However, if you choose to make an excuse by pointing fingers or adopting a victim mentality, there is not enough room created to grow.

Instead of making excuses for why things didn't work out, get curious and go into problem-solving mode. Failures can be used as opportunities to review your goal and objectives, but only if you take full responsibility.

4. You Stop Learning or Seeking Personal Growth

It is a trap to believe that you know everything about your goal. The truth is that you have only been exposed to a finite number of skills and knowledge, and there is so much more you can learn from reading books, taking courses, or listening to experts. When you stop learning or growing, your creativity dwindles and you approach challenges using the same tricks and strategies you know. This can be dangerous, especially when the types of challenges you encounter require innovative thinking.

The key is to see yourself as an eternal student, and the people and situations you encounter as teachers. Treat every problem, interaction, or life experience as a teachable moment, so your mind is constantly fed with new information to help you grow.

5. You Procrastinate

Another barrier that hinders progress is procrastination. This occurs when you know what needs to be done but delay doing it. Putting things off becomes a habit. For example, you might postpone a task to the evening, even though you had scheduled it for the morning. Eventually, you are forced to complete the task but have less time or energy available to do it. The result is rushed and poor-quality work that doesn't fulfill your objectives.

To address procrastination, you must confront the limiting beliefs that might cause you to delay your own progress. Reflect on some of the underlying fears or insecurities that may be at play. For instance, could you be afraid of running into obstacles you can't manage?

Or maybe feel a deep sense of inadequacy that makes you self-sabotage? Dealing with the underlying belief can remove the mental barrier and help you stay on track with your schedules.

HOW TO COPE WHEN THINGS DON'T GO ACCORDING TO PLAN

Let's face it—life can get in the way of our plans. Change and uncertainty are two uncontrollable factors that cannot be avoided, no matter how much preparation has been done. The COVID-19 pandemic, for example, brought about unprecedented change and a lot of uncertainty. Businesses shut down, new health scares emerged, and people could no longer socialize as usual.

Just imagine the impact of the pandemic on planning and goal setting. I can imagine that many small business owners needed to seek out loans and incur more debt to keep their businesses operating, since customers weren't allowed to leave their homes. I can also imagine how stressful it must have been for people who were adjusting to working from home, plus having to homeschool their children and make time for everyday household chores.

No matter how many times you have experienced setbacks, your ego gets a knock each time you fail. It can take a lot of time to bounce back from disappointment, but what's important to remember is that it is impossible. A failed plan is not a failed life. You can always go back to the drawing board and refine your goals. The strategies below can help to soften the blow after a setback and rebuild your confidence.

1. Acknowledge and Embrace Your Feelings

Think back to when you were a child and your ice cream fell on the floor, or you got yelled at by your parents. How did you feel at that moment? Were you sad, frustrated, or humiliated? When you experience setbacks as an adult, the same rush of emotions overtakes your body. The only difference is you don't allow yourself to acknowledge and embrace these strong emotions like you did when you were a child. As a result, you end up hurting and feeling physically, mentally, and emotionally unwell because of it.

Teach yourself to slow down whenever you feel emotionally triggered. Find a quiet room or area where you can sit alone and take a few minutes to acknowledge and embrace your strong emotions. Don't hold back from crying or yelling if that is how your anger wishes to be expressed. Your time alone can also be used to self-soothe and respond to your needs. Ask yourself: What can I do for myself right now? The answer may be to breathe, write in your journal, call a friend, recite positive affirmations, or revisit your purpose statement.

2. Accept the Reality for What It Is

Accepting reality means not fighting the current situation you are in. Indeed, you may not like where you are, or how others might have treated you, but you cannot change it either. Please don't confuse accepting reality with tolerating mediocrity or bad behaviors. You don't have to be proud of the way things are to be at peace with them. When you no longer feel the urge to resist changes in your life, you will notice that finding solutions to problems, or adapting to these changes, becomes so much easier.

3. Remain Flexible

When you are rigid in the face of adversity, the unexpected change feels painful. But if you can adapt to adversity, and find ways to navigate through the changes, you will be able to use the unfavorable circumstances to your advantage. Bruce Lee has a famous quote that explains the necessity of being flexible when confronted with challenges. He said (Donsky, 2020): "Be like water making its way through cracks. Do not be assertive, but adjust to the object, and you shall find a way around or through it. If nothing within you stays rigid, outward things will disclose themselves."

4. Challenge Your Perspective

Every situation can be seen from more than one perspective. What one person labels as a failure, another person will see as a blessing in disguise. It is, therefore, important to question whether you are looking at situations from an empowering or disempowering perspective. Challenge your beliefs and determine whether what you are thinking is helpful or harmful to your progress. For instance, will your belief about your most recent setback inspire you to wake up early in the morning and take charge of your day, or sleep until noon and procrastinate doing any goal-related tasks?

5. Determine What Is Within Your Control

It is normal to blame yourself when your plans don't work out. However, you may not always stop and consider whether the failed strategy was within your control or not. In your life, there are factors that you can control and change and others that you can neither control nor change. Factors within your control are governed by human effort. These include things like, following a schedule, setting goals, and working hard.

Factors outside of your control cannot be manipulated by human effort. These include things like the weather, economic crises, industry policy, and viruses and diseases.

Whenever you face a setback, reflect on the event and write a list of factors within and outside of your control. Focus your energy on the factors within your control, and look for ways to prevent the same mistakes from happening in the future. Accept the factors outside of your control, and realize that they affect millions of other people too.

WHY PERSEVERANCE IS THE KEY TO SUCCESS

Perseverance can be defined as the courage to continue taking action, despite the difficulty you may face along the way. What makes perseverance such a powerful quality is the fact that it relies on inner strength, not outer strength. Your inner strength is what keeps you focused and motivated to succeed, even when external circumstances look grim.

One of the ways you can develop perseverance is to rule out the possibility of quitting. Yes, that's right. Forget that quitting is even an option! This doesn't mean that you must continue to pursue a goal you have lost interest in. By all means, modify your goal until you are satisfied with the new direction it is taking you. Tell yourself that it is unacceptable to quit when:

- Other people are quitting.
- You are not achieving your goal quickly enough.
- You face new challenges that feel overwhelming.
- You don't receive support from friends and family.
- You doubt your ability to succeed.

The only time it is acceptable to stop working on your goals is when you have achieved them!

Another key component of development perseverance is being able to encourage yourself. There will be times when people and situations work against you, but you must remain stable in who you are. Don't allow yourself to be swayed by others' opinions, or be discouraged by an unexpected hurdle. Instead, remind yourself of previous times when you were able to rise above criticism, failure, frustrations, and any other emotion or experience that seeks to bring you down.

Below are a few journal prompts that can help you reflect on your display of perseverance:

1. Describe a past challenge that you have successfully overcome, which showcased one or a few of your strengths.

2. Describe a past situation that encouraged you to stand up for yourself. How did you feel afterward?

3. Describe a time when you pursued a goal you previously thought you could not achieve. What steps did you take to achieve this goal?

4. When you are feeling discouraged, what are five positive activities that uplift your spirit?

5. Think about three people in your life that display perseverance. How do these people inspire you on a daily basis?

6. Think about somebody in your life who you frequently clash with. It could be a difficult family member or coworker. Write down five things that you have in common with this person. It could be physical, mental, or emotional attributes.

7. What are three empowering beliefs that you continue to uphold, even when situations get tough?

8. Describe some of the activities that help you destress after a busy work day, or recharge your body.

EXERCISE: PLANNING CHECKLIST

Effective planning includes tools to measure progress. One of these tools is a planning checklist to ensure that you have completed every step that you need to do. The following checklist includes some of the planning elements we have discussed in this book. You are welcome to expand the checklist and include additional elements too!

Next to each component, indicate the status of the task (i.e., complete, in progress, not started) and add comments, if necessary.

Component	Status	Comments
Identifying core values.		
Drafting a purpose statement.		
Creating a SMART goal.		
Identifying strategic objectives.		
Drafting a weekly schedule.		
Cultivating a growth mindset.		
Monitoring progress on your goal.		

CHAPTER TAKEAWAYS

Executing the plan takes up the bulk of time on the road to success. This is due to the many twists and turns you will experience along the way. It is normal to fail several times when implementing your strategies. Many of the great inventors of all time failed thousands of times before finally discovering the winning formula. To avoid going back to your comfort zone, procrastinating, and being overcome with self-doubt, it is important mentally prepare for setbacks and develop perseverance.

Now that you have learned about how to execute your plan, let's move on to the next strategy for creating a successful plan—managing your priorities.

7

PRIORITY MANAGEMENT

Productivity is never an accident. It is always the result of a commitment to excellence, intelligent planning, and focused effort.

— PAUL J. MEYER

THE RELATIONSHIP BETWEEN PRIORITIZATION AND PLANNING

Planning is the ability to take a big idea, break it down into strategic objectives, and decide on which tasks are the most appropriate to achieve those objectives. A good plan will be specific because that is the only way you can ensure that your time is being spent wisely.

A useful skill that helps you determine what to include or remove from your plan is prioritization. In simple terms, prioritization is the ability to be resourceful. For example, instead of dividing your time between several tasks, you may choose two or three that are the most urgent or yield the most results, and carry them out to the best of your ability.

Having this ability to filter through tasks and select those that take the greatest priority can also improve your productivity in every aspect of your life. The truth of the matter is that you only have 24 hours in a day, and most of that time is spent sleeping, going to work, or eating meals. If you truly desire to find time for goal-related tasks, you will need to be more efficient in how you manage and complete everyday tasks. In other words, the more time you can save on everyday tasks, the more time you will have to work on your goals.

A sign that you are not prioritizing tasks correctly is treating every "want" the same way you treat a "need." Needs are non-negotiable tasks that are required to feel safe and healthy. They may include eating three meals a day, going to work, and spending time with family (i.e., if you are somebody who needs close relationships to feel safe and healthy). Needs automatically take priority and fill up most of your calendar because they impact your overall well-being.

Wants, on the other hand, are desires that can improve the quality of your life. The emphasis here is on the word "quality." You can still live a decent, healthy lifestyle without fulfilling every desire. For example, having an entry-level job might not be what you envision for your career, but it enables you to earn a living and pay bills. Ideally, your calendar should accommodate both needs and wants—however, a greater priority must be placed on needs being met.

When wants are given the same priority as needs, you will have less time to spend on tasks that are important for your stability and positive well-being. As a result, you will notice that although your lifestyle looks picture perfect, you feel physically exhausted, emotionally drained, and can't even take a moment to just breathe and check in with yourself.

Therefore, as much as prioritization and planning refer to two different concepts, they are two sides of the same coin. You cannot draft and carry out a plan without deciding which tasks take priority and are worth pursuing, and which ones aren't. You can start each week or month by sitting down and thinking about the areas of your life that you would like to focus on, and which related tasks take priority.

TIME MANAGEMENT MATRIX

Have you ever heard of the phrase, "putting first things first?" It means identifying and taking action on the most important tasks. As straightforward as that instruction sounds, it isn't always easy to decipher which tasks are more important than others, especially when all of them need to get done.

But since you only have a limited amount of time each day to carry out your tasks, how you spend each minute matters. Some tasks are worth sacrificing your morning for, while others can be postponed, or removed from your calendar completely. Thus, when thinking about which tasks to prioritize, remember that your time is limited, and how you spend it can be the difference between a productive and unproductive day.

A useful prioritization and time management tool that you can use is the Time Management Matrix. You may have read about it in Covey's book, *The 7 Habits of Highly Effective People,* but it was created by former U.S. President, Dwight D. Eisenhower. The matrix breaks down your daily tasks into four quadrants, based on their order of importance. Below is a summary of each quadrant:

Quadrant 1: Quadrant of Necessity—What Is Urgent and Important?

Ask yourself: *In my list of tasks, what is both urgent and important?* Crises and emergencies, like fixing a burst water heater at home, or completing a task with an impending deadline, will fall under this quadrant. Other examples of tasks that are a necessity include:

- responding to emails that can be life-changing (e.g., being prompt to respond to a recruiter)
- finding solutions to immediate problems (e.g., your car won't start, so you need to call a mechanic)
- responding to unexpected emergencies (e.g., your child's teacher phoned and requested to see you immediately)

It is important to not fall into the trap that many people fall into, which is to label every important task as an emergency. There are many tasks that are very important, but not something you need to drop everything for.

Quadrant 2: Quadrant of Quality and Personal Leadership–What Is Non-Urgent, But Important?

On a typical day, you will have tasks that are important, but not extremely urgent. These are usually the tasks we speak about when we are discussing prioritization. What matters to you might not matter to the next person; hence, the necessity of personal leadership. You will need to look at your diary and think about the tasks that reap the most rewards. Examples of tasks that fall under this quadrant include:

- building or sustaining meaningful relationships in your personal and professional life (e.g., setting an appointment to meet with your personal trainer)
- learning or practicing new skills (e.g., completing a short course)
- improving your physical, mental, and emotional health (e.g., taking 10 minutes in the evening to meditate)

To identify tasks that are important, but not urgent, it can help to think about what is most meaningful to you. Reflect on the goals you have written down and the life purpose you have discovered.

Quadrant 3: Quadrant of Deception—What Is Urgent, But Unimportant?

On the surface, Q3 and Q1 tasks look the same because they both create a sense of urgency. However, Q3 tasks are not important at all. For example, you might be looped into a meeting (urgency) that doesn't bring up anything of value to you (unimportant). Or your friend might ask you for a favor (urgent) that derails you from your day's agenda (unimportant). Other examples of urgent, but unimportant tasks include:

- email or notification interruptions (e.g., hearing an alert from your phone that turns out to be something of no value)
- spending a lot of time on a task that won't help you reach your goals (e.g., completing a presentation that is only due in a month)
- Responding to text messages from friends during work hours

The reason why this quadrant is called the quadrant of deception is that many of these tasks take up a lot of time, which means that you have less time to work on the really important tasks. To figure out if you are making good use of your time, ask yourself: *Is what I am doing moving me closer to my goal?*

Quadrant 4: Quadrant of Waste—What Is Non-Urgent and Unimportant?

The final quadrant includes tasks that are neither urgent nor important. We call these kinds of tasks time wasters. Even though these tasks aren't a productive way of spending your time, they do provide short-term gratification. For example, you might browse through social media for several hours out of boredom, curiosity, or the desire to instantly feel good. However, the pleasure is only for a moment, and in the long run, you may develop habits like procrastination, or dependency on digital devices. Examples of the tasks that fall under this quadrant include:

- gossiping with friends or coworkers
- mindlessly surfing the internet
- watching or keeping up with the news (to an excessive degree)

People who haven't yet discovered their purpose or clarified their goals tend to spend the majority of their time carrying out Q3 and Q4 tasks. It may be because they don't have objectives to reach for, or worthwhile tasks to structure their days around. A routine filled with Q3 and Q4 tasks can be detrimental to productivity, and open the door to unhealthy behaviors.

Now it's your turn! Write down a list of tasks you perform on a typical day.

Using the table below, group your daily tasks under each quadrant.

	Urgent	Non-Urgent
Important		
Unimportant		

Look at the completed table and reflect on how well you manage time. Are you putting first things first, and filling your day with important, non-urgent tasks? Or do you currently spend time on urgent, unimportant tasks?

The secret to prioritization and time management is knowing how to manage each quadrant effectively. Below are a few tips on how you can reorganize your tasks to ensure that your time is being spent on the most valuable tasks:

- **Quadrant 1 tasks**. Stop whatever you are doing and get them done as quickly as possible. Your objective is to respond to these tasks immediately so that they don't become too disruptive.
- **Quadrant 2 tasks**. Due to the amount of value that you get from working on these tasks, ensure that they fill up the majority of your day. Figure out your most productive times of the day (i.e., early in the morning, or late in the evening), and get as many of these tasks completed.
- **Quadrant 3 tasks**. Since these tasks are not urgent, delegate them to somebody else on your team or at home. Try to invest as little time as possible in them, until they become urgent (e.g., until the deadline for your report approaches).
- **Quadrant 4 tasks.** The best way to handle these tasks is to avoid them as much as possible. If you have scheduled them in your calendar,

remove them, and allocate that time to something more productive.

SNEAKY TIME WASTERS TO AVOID

According to research by Perlow et al. (2017) from the Harvard Business Review, executives spend close to 23 hours a week attending meetings. When you add it up, that is over 1,000 hours spent on meetings per year. Another study carried out by the same organization, surveyed 182 senior managers. The results showed that 71% of these managers believed that the meetings they frequently attend were unproductive (Perlow et al., 2017).

On a different front, a survey conducted by Ofcom (2020), which is the UK's communications regulatory body, found that the average person spends 6 hours and 25 minutes watching audiovisual content. That is nearly a full workday spent on the couch or the computer, consuming content.

In the section above, we explored what time wasters are (see Quadrant 4). However, sometimes, time wasters are not as blatantly obvious as gossiping with friends. Some sneaky time wasters appear to be a good use of your time, but in hindsight, you realize that there was no value gained from them.

Below are five examples of sneaky time wasters that can become major distractions, and tips on how to avoid them:

1. Unnecessary Meetings

Not all meetings that you are invited to are worth your time. Some of the factors that make a meeting unnecessary are when the agenda of the meeting doesn't concern you, when a meeting is created to make an announcement, or when there aren't clear talking points, which makes the meeting drag for a longer time.

How to avoid them: Get into the habit of asking the host, on the side, about the agenda of the meeting, before you accept the invite. If the meeting doesn't have an agenda or isn't relevant to you, politely decline. If you are the one scheduling meetings, make them shorter to allow participants to leave after 10, 15, or 20 minutes. Shorter meetings are often great for catch-ups, feedback sessions, reviewing progress, or conducting interviews.

2. Multitasking

The biggest productivity misconception is that multitasking can save you time. This is incorrect. In fact, multitasking can cause you to work slower and prevent you from being fully committed to any single task. When you multitask, your attention is divided among several different things, which makes it hard to focus on anyone.

How to avoid it: Focus on one task at a time. Start your day by working on the most important tasks, until you have scratched off your to-do list. When completing a task, take short 5–10 minutes restroom breaks after 15–30 minutes of intense focus. This kind of routine, or similar, can increase your concentration and delay tiredness.

3. Online Distractions

A sneaky time waster is finding an excuse to go online. Unless you are working on your computer, responding to emails, or conducting goal-related research, being online can be an unproductive way to spend your time. The biggest online distraction is social media, but keeping up with the latest world affairs, or browsing through online stores can be productivity killers too.

How to avoid them: There are several ways you can avoid online distractions. The first is to close all open tabs on your computer, besides the one you are working from. Secondly, log off social media accounts after every visit, and don't save your passwords on Google. This extra step makes the process of logging in more tedious, which can make you think twice about logging back on, each time. You can also adjust your phone or computer settings to restrict access to certain websites or set technology curfews each night where you put away all of your devices.

4. Interruptions

An interruption can be anything that causes you to lose focus on what you are doing. For instance, receiving a text message, or phone call, or being asked a question while you are working can distract you from your current task. Even though interruptions tend to be over in a matter of seconds, it is usually harder to regain focus once your "flow state" has been disturbed.

How to avoid them: The best way to avoid interruptions is to find an area or workspace that is strictly used for work purposes. If the area is open and other people are moving around, wear a pair of headphones to reduce the noise. Keep technological devices, like cell phones, out of sight, or at least put them on silent. Another great strategy is to find your most productive hours during the day and block them from your calendar (or set your status as "Unavailable" on work platforms).

5. Long To-Do Lists

To-do lists are useful planning tools to help you prioritize tasks. However, the bulkier a to-do list is, the less likely you are to complete all of the tasks. This may not seem like a big deal, but your brain certainly won't see it that way.

Whenever you complete a task, your brain releases dopamine, and you feel good about yourself. This boost of confidence is exactly what you need to get up the next morning and repeat the same routine. Failing to accomplish a task releases stress hormones, and you are likely to feel anxious or overwhelmed. Not completing your to-do list produces the same stress response as failing at something.

How to avoid them: For the sake of your productivity and motivation, it is better to create shorter lists consisting of the most important tasks. A list of between 3–7 tasks is enough to keep you busy throughout the day while leaving enough time for breaks.

You might be able to identify and remove time wasters from your calendar right now. But over time, you will be confronted with new time wasters that look different from what you are used to. So, how can you avoid time wasters in the future? Simple. Get into the habit of time blocking.

Time blocking is assigning chunks of time to specific tasks each day. This process is best completed in advance, so you can start each day knowing exactly how you will spend your time. You can also block out rest breaks in between your tasks to avoid distractions. For example, in between two back-to-back meetings, you can block out a 10-minute rest break to grab a coffee or mentally prepare for the next meeting.

EIGHT PRIORITIZATION AND PRODUCTIVITY TECHNIQUES

Productivity hacks that work for one person are not always suitable for another. An essential part of increasing your productivity is learning what works for you, and doing that consistently. You may even find that combining two techniques works better than committing to a single one. The aim is to find your winning formula, so you can improve how you prioritize tasks and manage your time. Below are eight prioritization and productivity techniques to consider:

1. Pareto's 80/20 Rule

Pareto's Principle states that roughly 80% of the outcomes are a result of 20% of the inputs (Tardi, 2019). For example, if you had a list of 10 tasks to complete in a day, only 2 of those tasks would be considered high-priority tasks (those that yield the most benefits). You can practice Pareto's Principle whenever you want to decide which tasks to start with first.

2. Get the Hard Tasks Completed During Productive Hours

Some people choose to start their day working on hard tasks. However, since hard tasks require a lot of brain power, they can take up a lot of time. Instead of starting your day with hard tasks, schedule them during your most productive hours. This could be between 5:00–8:00 a.m., 10:00–12:00 p.m., or the late hours of the evening. During your most productive hours, you can achieve hyperfocus and work a lot efficiently on hard tasks.

3. The Ivy Lee Method

Every evening, before you go to sleep, write down six important tasks that you need to complete tomorrow. Organize them in the order of importance, from the most to the least important. It might help to apply other useful strategies like the time management matrix and time blocking to organize your tasks.

The following day, begin with the most important task, then once you have completed it, move on to the second most important task, and so forth. Only after you have completed all six tasks can you move on to any other task you need to accomplish. Repeat the process in the evening, writing down six priority tasks you need to accomplish. If you were not able to complete all six tasks by the end of the day, begin the next day where you left off.

4. The 1–3–5 Rule

Every evening, before you go to sleep, write down one big task, three medium tasks, and five small tasks that you can accomplish tomorrow. If you have a very busy schedule, you can modify the rule and write down one big task, two medium tasks, and three small tasks that you need to accomplish. The aim is to reduce the number of tasks that you are focusing on each day to boost productivity and limit distractions.

5. Pomodoro Technique

A pomodoro is the amount of time spent intensely focusing on a task. An average pomodoro is 25 minutes in length; however, you can shorten yours to 10- or 15-minute intervals. Practicing the technique is simple. Pick a task that you can break down into 25-minute intervals. Set a stopwatch for 25 minutes. When the timer rings, step away from your desk, and take a short break (you are welcome to time your breaks too). After the break, start the stopwatch again and complete another cycle.

6. The One-Minute Rule

Look at your to-do list and identify tasks that you can accomplish in less than a minute. Complete those tasks immediately! Examples of tasks that can be done in less than a minute include responding to an email, making a phone call, and 50 jumping jacks. This rule is great to use when you have a lot of small tasks to do.

7. Time Tracking

Time tracking is the process of monitoring how long it takes you to complete certain tasks. The purpose of this technique is to improve your time management skills and hold yourself accountable for the time allocated to certain activities. All you need to begin is a stopwatch and an Excel spreadsheet (you can also download a free time-tracking app). Write down your list of tasks in one column, and the start and stop times in the next two columns. You can start tracking your time for a day, then track it over a week. Over time, you will start to notice a pattern.

8. Planning With 168 Hours

Like most people, you create routines based on the 24-hour clock. This means that if you really want to get tasks done, you need to find a way of scheduling them into your 24-hour day. But what would happen if you created routines based on the 168 hours you have in a week? Wouldn't that free up the congestion of your day and help you spread out tasks? You can use the 168-hour rule to create a productive weekly schedule. A great technique to use alongside this rule is time tracking.

OPTIMIZING YOUR CALENDAR

Apart from a diary or to-do list, you can manage your time more efficiently by creating a calendar. Nowadays, creating a calendar is as simple as using the calendar feature that comes with your email account, or downloading a calendar app. The perks of having a digital calendar are that you can color code different tasks, use the time-blocking technique more effectively, and automate reminders minutes, hours, or days before important events.

There are two ways to design your calendar. The first is a more traditional approach, where the day is divided into 60-minute intervals. Single tasks can be blocked off for some hours (e.g., blocking off eight hours spent at work), but smaller tasks, like taking a rest break, often get overlooked. Designing your calendar using this approach is useful if your days tend to consist of the same recurring tasks.

The second approach is more flexible. Here, the typical hour is broken down into 10-, 15-, and 30-minute intervals. For example, in the space of an hour, you can schedule a 15-minute Zoom meeting, followed by a 45-minute gym session. Breaking down tasks by the hour is useful when your daily tasks and commitments change regularly.

After deciding which design to go for, you are ready to optimize your calendar. But first, think about what you are optimizing for. For instance, do you want to optimize your calendar to buy back time? Want to prioritize your goals? Or get enough breaks in between tasks? Getting clear on why you want to optimize your calendar will help you decide on which tasks to prioritize each day, and how much time to allocate for them.

The next step is looking for tasks that you can delegate, automate, or remove from your calendar. If you are part of a social group, like working in a team, living with your family, or being part of a network of friends, it is acceptable to ask for help. Identify those tasks that are general enough for someone else to do, like washing the dishes or attending a meeting on your behalf, and delegate them to someone else. Be willing to return the favor when others come to you for help too!

Take another look at your to-do list and find tasks that you can automate. If you go online, you will find an app or software for just about any task under the sun. And even when the app or software doesn't exist, you can hire a virtual assistant. There are a few questions to ask yourself when deciding on which tasks to automate:

- What tasks do you perform repeatedly?
- What tasks don't require complex thinking or emotional intelligence?
- What tasks can be performed faster by a machine?

These few tips will assist you in optimizing your calendar. But you are also welcome to download digital tools that will take care of the syncing, organizing, and optimization for you. Below are just some of the tools available online:

- **Shift**: A desktop app that allows you to add all of your favorite apps, websites, and workflow tools under one centralized platform. Your workstation makes accessing various accounts easier, without having to browse online.
- **Airtable**: This platform allows you to integrate multiple calendars into one centralized account. This streamlines the process of viewing different calendars, such as your

personal and work calendar, and receiving task reminders in one place.

- **Sunsama**: A useful tool that can help you focus on priority tasks by pulling a variety of tasks from other apps, and setting daily, weekly, or monthly goals. The tasks that you aren't able to complete today are automatically pushed to tomorrow, which helps you stay on track.
- **Motion**: A tool that is built on artificial intelligence (AI), which helps you build a schedule. To begin, the app requires access to your calendars. Thereafter, you can customize your schedule with existing and any additional tasks. Finally, the built-in algorithm prioritizes your tasks for you!
- **Reclaim**: If you are having trouble with time blocking, this simple tool can assist you. It can create, organize, and block off tasks on your calendar, as well as optimize your schedule based on what needs to get done first.

Optimizing your calendar isn't a once-off or one-day activity. To create an optimized calendar, you need to first think about what you want to achieve. For instance, how do you want your calendar to improve your focus, well-being, or productivity? Thereafter, you can look at your daily tasks and decide on which ones to add to your calendar. Remember, there aren't enough time slots to schedule every task. There are some tasks that you will need to delegate, automate, and remove from your list. If you struggle along the way, there are plenty of digital tools that can help you create an organized and optimized calendar.

EXERCISE: MOSCOW METHOD

One of the common threats to productivity is treating everything like a priority. You might tell yourself that you must complete the long list of requirements for the day, even though there are only two or three non-negotiable tasks. The MoSCoW method helps you rethink your priorities and assign tasks under four categories:

- **Must have**: These are tasks that are mandatory to complete, otherwise you will suffer negative consequences.
- **Should have**: These are tasks that aren't mandatory, but can improve the quality of your life, or help you achieve goals.

- **Could have**: These are desirable tasks, and probably on your bucket list or wish list, but aren't necessary.
- **Won't have**: These tasks might bring short-term gratification, but in the long run, you are better off not engaging in them.

Write down a list of your daily tasks below, then sort them under the four categories in the following table.

Now it's your turn! Write down a list of tasks you perform on a typical day.

In the table below, group them using the MoSCoW method.

Must Have	**Should Have**
Could Have	**Won't Have**

CHAPTER TAKEAWAYS

Prioritization is an essential part of planning. It allows you to focus on what you need to do to achieve your daily objectives. Not every task is important, even if it may be urgent! There are many urgent, but unimportant tasks that can fill up your diary and lower your levels of productivity. The hallmark of a productive day is not necessarily getting everything done, but instead getting the *right things* done.

Now that you have learned about how to prioritize your schedule, let's move on to the final strategy for creating a successful plan—keeping yourself motivated.

8

EXTRINSIC MOTIVATION? INTRINSIC MOTIVATION? OR BOTH?

You are your master. Only you have the master keys to open the inner locks.

— AMIT RAY

STALLONE'S JOURNEY TO SUCCESS

Sylvester Stallone moved to California with his wife to pursue his dream of becoming an actor. What neither of them could anticipate are the many setbacks that he would experience along the journey. Most of his resources were spent attending auditions. But one after the other, he got rejected. At his lowest point, Stallone was unable to buy food or pay his rent and ended up sleeping at the local bus station for three days.

One day, he caught a match between Chuck Wepner and Muhammad Ali playing on TV. This match inspired him to write a movie script about a retired boxer who gets back into the ring and fights a heavyweight champion. He called the movie *Rocky* and believed that he would do a great job starring as the main character.

Stallone approached a studio to sell his script. He didn't care about how much money he would get paid, as long as he played the role of Rocky. The studio refused to cast Stallone in the film, citing that he didn't have the right look. They wanted a "real actor," not an amateur.

As disappointed as he was, Stallone never backed down. After every rejection, he returned home with his script, hoping to one day get his big break. To his surprise, the studio kept reaching out to him, each time offering him more money for the script. The answer was still no, and there was no way around it. Finally, they agreed on a settlement: $35,000 for the script, and Stallone could play the role of Rocky.

The movie was a huge success! It won awards for Best Directing, Best Picture, and Best Film Editing at the

Oscars. The main actor, Stallone, was nominated for best actor, and he went on to have a successful movie career.

Stallone's journey to success highlights the importance of a key factor in planning and executing your goals—motivation. Motivation can be described as the reason for doing certain activities or living in a particular way. Stallone endured a lot of hardship because he was motivated to become an actor. Without having such a strong internal desire, who knows how far he would've made it on his journey?

INTRINSIC VS. EXTRINSIC MOTIVATION

Have you ever considered what drives your actions? For instance, what drives you to go to work, maintain strong bonds with your family, or decide to start a business? Motivation is the blanket term used to explain why individuals behave in certain ways. Psychologists have gone a step further and identified two types of motivation that affect human desire. These are known as intrinsic and extrinsic motivations.

Intrinsic motivation refers to motivation that comes from within. The three elements that make up intrinsic motivation are a sense of purpose, autonomy, and mastery. For example, you might be motivated by gaining independence, completing meaningful work, or becoming a better version of yourself.

One of the defining factors of intrinsic motivation is the ability to take action without any promise of external rewards. You might decide to quit your day job and start a business because you are passionate about entrepreneurship, even though your financial success is not guaranteed. In other words, you are inspired to live a certain way because you find meaning in doing so.

This doesn't mean that intrinsically motivated behaviors cannot bring external rewards. In some cases, they can. However, the true payoff is in the way those behaviors enhance your physical, mental, and emotional well-being.

There are five factors that increase intrinsic motivation:

- **The desire for a challenge**. Setting and chasing after goals can give your life a sense of meaning, and promote personal growth. The trick though is setting goals that provide just enough of a challenge to move you out of your comfort zone, but not feel overwhelming.
- **The desire for control**. As part of gaining security and independence, you will naturally desire to have more control over your mind,

body, emotions, finances, habits, environment, and so much more. This desire can inspire important life decisions, like quitting smoking, changing jobs, planning for retirement, and so on.

- **The desire for recognition**. Some achievements are worthwhile because of how they raise your status. For example, you can be motivated to pursue a goal because of the recognition you will get from your peers.

Extrinsic motivation, on the other hand, refers to motivation that comes from external rewards, symbols, or achievements. In other words, you are motivated by the hopes of making money, expanding your professional network, losing weight, or graduating from university. Unlike intrinsic motivation where the motivation to complete a task comes from an inner desire or purpose, you are motivated by achieving or obtaining tangible results.

For example, you may not enjoy waking up at 5:00 a.m. and running around your neighborhood, but you do it nonetheless because of the promise of getting fit. For any extrinsically motivated behavior to be worthwhile, there must be some type of reward you get from practicing it. Below are a few examples of extrinsically motivated behaviors:

- working an extra shift at work to earn more wages at the end of the month
- studying a skills-based course to obtain a certificate
- going to the gym four times a week to reach your fitness goal
- saving money so that you can put a down payment on your dream house

There is a tendency for some people to perceive extrinsic motivation as shallow and intrinsic motivation as noble. However, both types of motivation are useful and effective in bettering your life and achieving meaningful goals. Moreover, the kind of goals you pursue determine which type of motivation would be more appropriate.

For example, if your goal is to adopt healthy habits, intrinsically motivated behaviors may be appropriate. However, if you desire to achieve financial stability, then extrinsically motivated behaviors would be most suitable. Understanding how each motivator works and how they can drive behavioral changes can improve your performance and commitment to tasks.

THE SIX STAGES OF BEHAVIORAL CHANGE

If you have ever attempted to pursue a goal, you will know that change doesn't happen overnight. In fact, any kind of goal that requires you to learn new behaviors can come with its own set of challenges. Human beings are creatures of habit, which means that we prefer things to stay the same. The process of unlearning behaviors and adopting new ones can be a shock to our system; thus, requiring us to be more patient with our slow progress.

Some people can easily adjust to change, while others need a lot more time. Three factors that can either delay or accelerate an individual's responsiveness to change are:

- **Being ready for change**. Having the motivation, resources, and effective plan to embrace change successfully.
- **Discovering obstacles that delay or prevent change**. Experiencing physical, mental, or environmental barriers that make it difficult or impossible to embrace change.
- **Likelihood of returning to old habits**. Without adopting healthy coping mechanisms, it can be difficult to remain resilient during tough times along the journey.

To explain the process of how people gradually change their behaviors, researchers Carlo DiClemente and James Prochaska came up with the Stages of Change Model, during a study to help participants quit smoking (Cherry, 2021). The researchers identified six stages of behavioral change that occur gradually. Relapses were seen as an inevitable reality during the process of behavioral change, but over time, individuals showed more commitment.

Below is an outline of each stage and tips on how to successfully manage it:

Stage 1: Pre-Contemplation

The pre-contemplation stage is where everyone begins. During this stage, you are unaware of the problem or need for change. The thought of changing your behaviors doesn't cross your mind, or if it does, you are in denial of the impact of your behaviors.

How to manage: Self-reflection can be useful during this stage. If you have a journal, you can explore a few questions about the need for change. Here are a few journal prompts to explore:

- What do I recognize about myself that I am afraid to accept?
- What am I afraid of?/Who am I afraid of?

- What are the signs that I might have a problem?

Stage 2: Contemplation

Once you have recognized the need for change, you will be ushered into the contemplation stage. During this stage, you are more open to learning more about your need or problem and various ways to address it. A good sign of openness is starting to embrace the benefits of making change. However, that doesn't rule out your fears. It is common to go back and forth between committing to change and staying in your comfort zone; this back and forth can continue for several months or years.

How to manage: To feel comfortable with the idea of changing your behaviors, weigh the pros and cons of maintaining your existing behaviors. Create two lists and compare the costs and benefits.

You can also identify any mental or physical barriers that may be stopping you from embracing change fully. For example, you may be afraid of failure, or not have enough resources to invest in the change. Working on these barriers can increase your readiness for change.

Stage 3: Preparation

The preparation stage is when you begin to take action. Bear in mind, you may still feel internal resistance to change, or experience frequent relapses. Your ability to encourage yourself and celebrate the small changes is what will keep you motivated during this stage.

How to manage: The more planning you do, the less anxious you will feel about being proactive. Create SMART goals, build your roadmap, and plan for worst-case scenarios. Revise your plans regularly, so that you can maintain consistent progress.

Stage 4: Action

All of the preparation and planning leads to the action stage. If you have completed thorough planning, you will have a detailed step-by-step guide on how to accomplish your goal. Oftentimes, action is slowed down because of poor planning—including planning for unforeseen setbacks. Another reason for little action is not having a strong enough "why" to keep you going through the low moments.

How to manage: Be your own cheerleader. Reward yourself for small daily wins, like completing all of your tasks, or successfully avoiding temptation. It is also important to evaluate your environment and make sure that you are spending time in places where you can be productive, or with people who are positive influences.

Stage 5: Maintenance

Many people think that taking action is the hardest part of changing behavior, but maintaining the change is. Finding ways to make the new behaviors sustainable in the long term is not easy, especially when you haven't changed your environment. To make the change long-lasting, assess your habits, how you spend your time and the strategies you have enforced to avoid old behaviors.

How to manage: Create checks and balances to hold yourself accountable. These might include joining a social or support group of like-minded people with similar interests, optimizing your calendar (refer to Chapter 7), setting manageable goals, and creating a relapse plan with positive coping strategies.

Stage 6: Relapse

The relapse stage may occur once new behaviors have been incorporated into your lifestyle, or throughout the various stages. When a relapse happens, you may feel frustrated, humiliated, or disappointed. How you deal with the relapse is what determines how quickly you can bounce back.

How to manage: Identify the triggers that lead to relapses. For example, do you often get tempted to cheat on your diet whenever you eat at a restaurant? Or, skip a few days of working out when you don't feel confident about yourself? Get to know your triggers and create a plan on how to handle them, before they grow out of proportion.

When you approach any goal with the understanding that your behavior will change gradually, and relapses are likely to occur, you can prepare for each stage of the journey.

TECHNIQUES TO KEEP YOURSELF MOTIVATED

It is normal to lose motivation during the process of achieving your goals. This is especially common when working on long-term goals. Staying motivated will require a little bit of effort and creativity on your part. Fortunately, there are some powerful techniques that can pull you out of a slump, revive your enthusiasm, and get you back on track!

Below are a few motivational techniques to consider.

Positive Affirmations

Positive affirmations are empowering statements that recognize your potential, strengths, and efforts to change. Reciting positive affirmations can improve your moods, increase your confidence, and in the long term, help you adjust your beliefs about yourself. Writing positive affirmations is simple. Make sure that your statements are written in the present tense and use positive words like "can" rather than "can't." An example of a positive affirmation is: *I am stronger than I was yesterday.*

Below are a few positive affirmations that you can recite before you start each day:

- I am open to learning something new today.
- I am allowed to be happy.
- I am capable of balancing my work and personal life.
- I can achieve the goals I set for myself.
- I am responsible for my life.
- I embrace mistakes and know they are part of the journey to success.
- I am a positive influence on others.
- I deserve to be around positive people.

Now, it's your turn! Write down a list of positive affirmations to add to the list above.

Asking for Feedback

Asking for honest feedback can boost your motivation because it allows you to consider your life from a different perspective. The people closest to you may hold certain beliefs and opinions about you that can lead to introspection and positive change. The art of effective feedback is about finding the right people (those who are personally invested in your well-being) and preparing the right questions. Below are a few suggestions on questions to ask:

- What is a strength that is obvious about me?
- What am I doing well right now that I should continue doing?
- How do I contribute to the lives of others?

- What areas of growth have you identified in my life?
- What are some of the behaviors I can improve?
- What makes our relationship work?
- What recent positive change have you noticed about me?
- What is something that I don't give myself credit for?

Asking Yourself Open-Ended Questions

Open-ended questions create room for exploration. You can look beyond what you already know about yourself, and discover new thoughts or feelings that can trigger change. These types of questions can also reignite passion and remind you of why you started pursuing your goal in the first place. The best way to answer open-ended questions is through journaling. Below are a few open-ended questions you can explore about your goals:

1. What three lessons have you learned so far while pursuing your goal?

2. What actions are you currently taking that are working?

3. What are three powerful habits that have kept you committed to your goal?

4. Are you receiving enough support from friends and family?

5. What are some of the concerns you have about achieving your goal?

6. Has your definition of success changed from when you started working on your goal, until this point?

7. What inner desires does your goal fulfill?

8. What are five steps you can take to improve performance on goal-related tasks?

9. Where do you see yourself in the next 10 years? Describe an ideal day, 10 years from now.

10. Describe a life event that has motivated you to desire positive change in your life.

Cognitive Restructuring

Sometimes, the reason behind feeling discouraged is the quality of your thoughts. Cognitive restructuring is a cognitive behavioral therapy (CBT) technique that allows you to examine and challenge your thoughts to make them more balanced and fair. This technique aims to confront errors in thinking and provide alternative responses to problems or situations.

A common way to practice cognitive restructuring is to challenge your assumptions, more especially those that cause you to be resistant to change or create a mental barrier (i.e., believing that you aren't capable of developing a skill). To challenge your assumptions, you can ask yourself open-ended questions, and see whether your thoughts are logical or biased. Questions may include:

- Does this thought match reality? Is it an indication of what I see happening right now?
- Does this thought validate my feelings, rather than validating the facts?
- What other perspectives am I not seeing?
- Could I be using past information to interpret what is happening right now?
- Could I be seeing the situation as black-or-white, when in reality it is more complicated?
- What are the positive and negative outcomes of believing this assumption?
- How does this assumption affect the people around me?
- How does this assumption improve or slow down my progress?

Cognitive restructuring can also be used to adjust negative self-talk. We can define self-talk as how you speak to yourself. Negative self-talk refers to harmful beliefs or expectations that you hold and repeat about yourself. When pursuing your goal, these beliefs and expectations can interfere with your performance.

A cognitive restructuring technique to challenge negative self-talk is to respond with "yes, and… " rather than rejecting the thought or buying into it. Doing this can help you validate your feelings, rather than shutting them out. It can also teach you to have a balanced view of your life; seeing things as not merely good or bad, but a combination of both.

Practicing the "yes, and… " technique is simple. Whenever you notice a negative thought directed at yourself, stop and say "yes, and… " followed by facts or a truth that can set your mind at ease. For example, when you think, "I always quit too soon," you can respond with, "Yes, and every day I practice holding myself accountable to my goals." Or when self-doubt causes you to say, "I'm not worthy of being successful," you can respond with, "Yes, and my feelings of unworthiness won't stop me from improving the quality of my life."

Use the space below to practice correcting negative self-talk with the "yes, and… " technique.

EXERCISE: VISUALIZING YOUR IDEAL FUTURE

Find a quiet area or room where you can spend 20 minutes by yourself. Switch off your devices or put them on "Do not disturb." Sit down on a comfortable chair and close your eyes. Spend a few minutes focusing on your breath. Take full and deep breaths, inhaling through your nose and exhaling out your mouth.

When you are ready, imagine that you are transported into the future. You can decide on how far into the future you would like to go (e.g., traveling 5, 10, or 15 years into the future). As you familiarize yourself with this improved way of living, reflect on the following questions:

- What does success look like?
- Who are some of the people around me?
- What is my occupation?
- Where do I live?
- How do I spend my day?
- What do I value in life?
- How do I feel about myself?

Enjoy the mental images that are created in your mind. Pretend as though you were there and living through each moment. Check-in with your body and notice how you feel. You can also write down words or phrases that appear in your mind during the visualization. When you are ready, take a deep breath, and open your eyes.

CHAPTER TAKEAWAYS

Motivation is what keeps you going when the journey toward achieving your goals gets tough. Depending on the type of goal you are pursuing, you might rely on intrinsic or extrinsic motivation. Both types of motivation are effective in boosting your performance and positively changing behaviors. It is also worth emphasizing that feeling discouraged is normal. Due to the nature of the obstacles you are faced with, you won't always feel strong or capable. The good news is that there are many ways to motivate yourself and get out of the slump, like reciting positive affirmations, asking for feedback, asking yourself open-ended questions, or challenging your thoughts.

CONCLUSION

Unless commitment is made, there are only promises and hopes; but no plans.

— PETER F. DRUCKER

The journey to success is not a straight path. There are many twists and turns along the road; some that you were able to anticipate and others that you didn't see coming. The fact that there is so much that can go wrong on your way to success makes planning essential!

It is understandable that you may not have time to carry out the type of extensive planning we have discussed in this book. The fast-paced nature of modern life makes it difficult to juggle everyday responsibilities and pursuing meaningful goals. However, part of the creativity required in planning involves improving your time management, so you can *find* time.

Imagine if you were to drive to a new destination without a map. Not only would that journey take much longer, but it would also be extremely risky. In the same way, planning is the roadmap that you carry with you whenever you decide to pursue a goal. It details the purpose of the journey, objectives to achieve along the way, and daily tasks that can keep you on track.

Many components go into strategically planning for success. Throughout this book, you have been exposed to many of them. Some of these components include discovering your big "Why?" creating SMART goals, clarifying your objectives, adjusting your mindset, executing and reviewing your plan, as well as improving your time management.

You can increase your chances of success by simply spending more time on creating a powerful plan. The strategies and techniques provided in this book will help you set a good foundation.

If you have enjoyed reading this book, please leave a review.

REFERENCES

Ackoff, R. (1981). *4 approaches to planning (reactive, inactive, preactive, and proactive).* Entarga. https://www.entarga.com/stratplan/approaches.htm

Ahmer, A. (2018, October 3). *Importance of planning in life.* Medium. https://medium.com/@anumahmer21/importance-of-planning-in-our-life-c756625db0b2

Babauta, L. (n.d.). *The ultimate guide to motivation–How to achieve any goal.* Zen Habits. https://zenhabits.net/the-ultimate-guide-to-motivation-how-to-achieve-any-goal/

Beard, C. (2019, February 25). *How to plan your weekly schedule for success.* The Blissful Mind. https://theblissfulmind.com/how-to-plan-your-week/

Benson, D. (2018, March 7). *7 reasons why making a plan is the key to success.* Diane Benson. http://www.dianebenson.co.uk/7-reasons-why-making-plan-key-success/

Bradley, A. K. (2021, January 17). *How to successfully manage multiple goals at once.* AK Bradley. https://akbradley.com/2021/01/17/how-to-successfully-manage-multiple-goals-at-once/

Buchanan, A. (2017, March 16). *The nature of mindsets.* Medium. https://medium.com/benefit-mindset/the-nature-of-mindsets-18afba2ac890e

Bundrant, M. (2019, February 7). *9 ways to prepare for change and live your dream life.* Lifehack. https://www.lifehack.org/822913/prepare-for-change

Caldwell, J. (2020, April 22). *How to cope when your plans don't go as expected.* 360 Youth Services. https://360youthservices.org/tips-on-how-to-cope-when-your-plans-dont-go-as-expected/

Celes. (2008, December 28). *Put first things first.* Personal Excellence. https://personalexcellence.co/blog/put-first-things-first/

Cherry, K. (2019, September 27). *Understanding intrinsic motivation.*

Verywell Mind. https://www.verywellmind.com/what-is-intrinsic-motivation-2795385

Cherry, K. (2020, January 15). *Extrinsic vs. intrinsic motivation: What's the difference?* Verywell Mind. https://www.verywellmind.com/differences-between-extrinsic-and-intrinsic-motivation-2795384

Cherry, K. (2021a, April 13). *What is extrinsic motivation?* Verywell Mind. https://www.verywellmind.com/what-is-extrinsic-motivation-2795164

Cherry, K. (2021b, July 28). *The 6 stages of behavior change.* Verywell Mind. https://www.verywellmind.com/the-stages-of-change-2794868

Colan, L. (2016, September 6). *Getting to know fear.* Inc.Africa. https://incafrica.com/library/lee-colan-getting-to-know-fear

Connors, C. (2017, March 23). *The 4 stages of success.* CNBC. https://www.cnbc.com/2017/03/23/the-4-stages-of-success.html

Davis, T. (n.d.). *Mindsets: Definition, examples and books on mindset (Growth, fixed and other types).* The Berkeley Well-Being Institute. https://www.berkeleywellbeing.com/mindsets.html

Debevoise, N. D. (2021, January 26). *The third critical step in problem solving that Einstein missed.* Forbes. https://www.forbes.com/sites/nelldebevoise/2021/01/26/the-third-critical-step-in-problem-solving-that-einstein-missed/?sh=7bfa37063807

Donsky, D. (2020, July 29). *We are like water...* Medium. https://debdonsky.medium.com/we-are-like-water-f89372f45bc2

Dowches-Wheeler, J. (2022, February 21). *How to find your life purpose in 4 easy steps.* Bright Space Coaching. https://www.brightspacecoaching.com/blog/find-your-purpose

Eby, K. (2019, January 9). *The essential guide to writing SMART goals.* Smartsheet. https://www.smartsheet.com/blog/essential-guide-writing-smart-goals

Emerson, C. (2022, June 29). *Calendar optimization: 28 scheduling hacks to save time and stay organized.* SavvyCal. https://savvycal.com/articles/calendar-optimization/

Escar, E. (2022, July 16). *How many hours a day can a human actually work? (What science recommends!).* Iris Reading. https://irisreading.

com/how-many-hours-a-day-can-a-human-actually-work-what-science-recommends/

Ghete, P. (2020, January 8). *Why you need clarity for success - and how to get it (7).* Paula Ghete. https://paulaghete.com/why-you-need-clarity-for-success-7/

Giolando, E. (2020, June 19). *3 best things to do when you have too many goals.* The Muse. https://www.themuse.com/advice/3-practical-things-to-do-when-you-have-too-many-goals

Goodreads. (n.d.-a). *Steve Maraboli quote.* https://www.goodreads.com/author/show/4491185.Steve_Maraboli

Goodreads. (n.d.-b). *Tim Fargo quotes* (Author of alphabet success - Keeping it simple. My secrets to success.). https://www.goodreads.com/author/quotes/7246141.Tim_Fargo

Goodreads. (2019). *A quote by Henry Ford.* https://www.goodreads.com/quotes/978-whether-you-think-you-can-or-you-think-you-can-t--you-re

Goodreads. (2020). *Amit Ray quote.* https://www.goodreads.com/author/show/492884.Amit_Ray

Guest, R. (2019, August 14). *Why failing to plan really does mean planning to fail.* Royston Guest. https://www.roystonguest.com/blog/why-failing-to-plan-really-does-mean-planning-to-fail-2/

Haughey, D. (2014, December 13). *A brief history of SMART goals.* Project Smart. https://www.projectsmart.co.uk/smart-goals/brief-history-of-smart-goals.php

Houston, E. (2019, April 9). *What is goal setting and how to do it well.* PositivePsychology.com. https://positivepsychology.com/goal-setting/

Jen. (2022, July 16). *75 awesome growth mindset quotes for kids.* Reluctant Homeschool Mama. https://www.reluctanthomeschoolmama.com/growth-mindset-quotes-for-kids/

Kirkus. (2012). *Dream big: Michael Jordan and the pursuit of excellence.* [Review of the book *Dream big: Michael Jordan and the pursuit of excellence,* by D. Jordan]. https://www.kirkusreviews.com/book-reviews/deloris-jordan/dream-big-michael-jordan-pursuit-olympic-gold/

Kristenson, S. (2022, January 1). *37 personal purpose statement examples and ideas.* Happier Human. https://www.happierhuman.com/personal-purpose-statements/

Landau, C. (n.d.). *16 effective prioritization and time management strategies.* HourStack. https://hourstack.com/blog/16-effective-prioritization-and-time-management-strategies

Layla. (2020, January 30). *The 5 stages of achieving your goal and how to overcome them.* Shut Up & Achieve. https://shutupandachieve.com/the-5-stages-of-achieving-your-goal-how-to-overcome-them/

Leal, C. J. (2021, April 9). *The formula to finding purpose: How to find your ikigai.* Kanban Zone. https://kanbanzone.com/2021/the-formula-to-finding-purpose-how-to-find-your-ikigai/

Lim, S. (2019, November 21). *Why having a sense of purpose is important to succeed in life.* Stunning Motivation. https://stunningmotivation.com/purpose-is-important/

Lim, S. (2022, June 16). *10 things that hinder your growth and progress in life.* Stunning Motivation. https://stunningmotivation.com/things-that-hinder-your-growth-and-progress-in-life/

Locke, R. (2015, May 21). *The stories of these 5 athletes will motivate everyone of you.* Lifehack; Lifehack. https://www.lifehack.org/articles/communication/the-stories-these-5-athletes-will-motivate-everyone-you.html

Lottery Guru. (n.d.). *Lotto America IA.* https://lotteryguru.com/united-states-lottery-results/us-lotto-america-ia

Lucidchart. (2017, November 29). *The 5 steps of the strategic planning process.* https://www.lucidchart.com/blog/5-steps-of-the-strategic-planning-process

Malone-Kircher, M. (2016, November 22). *James Dyson on the 5,126 vacuums that didn't work and the one that finally did.* The Vindicated. https://nymag.com/vindicated/2016/11/james-dyson-on-5-126-vacuums-that-didnt-work-and-1-that-did.html

Matveyeva, A. (2021, July 28). *101 productivity quotes to keep you inspired at work.* Chanty. https://www.chanty.com/blog/productivity-quotes/

Mayberry, M. (2017, January 18). *10 great quotes on the power of goals.*

Entrepreneur. https://www.entrepreneur.com/leadership/10-great-quotes-on-the-power-of-goals/287411

Mercurio, Z. (2016, June 1). *25 essential quotes on the power of a purpose.* Zach Mercurio. https://www.zachmercurio.com/2016/06/25-quotes-on-the-power-of-a-purpose/

Morero, C. (2018, September 14). *Why you should create a timeline for your goals.* Saturday Gift. https://www.saturdaygift.com/create-a-timeline-for-your-goals/

Muguku, D. (2017, February 24). *9 tips on how to persevere in order to succeed.* ThriveYard. https://www.thriveyard.com/9-tips-on-how-to-persevere-in-order-to-succeed/

Nature Crafts. (2010, May 14). *A short story on the importance of planning ahead.* Naturecrafts's Blog. https://naturecrafts.wordpress.com/2010/05/14/a-short-story-on-the-importance-of-planning-ahead/

Ofcom. (2020). *Media nations 2020: UK report.* https://www.ofcom.org.uk/__data/assets/pdf_file/0010/200503/media-nations-2020-uk-report.pdf

Perlow, L. A., Hadley, C. N., & Eun, E. (2017, July 1). *Stop the meeting madness.* Harvard Business Review. https://hbr.org/2017/07/stop-the-meeting-madness

Pogue, S. (2019, March 7). *45 powerful planning quotes to help you reach your goals.* Workzone. https://www.workzone.com/blog/project-planning-quotes/

Priambodo, B. (2020, June 10). *3 hours is all you need to achieve success.* Phase. https://phase.com/magazine/3-hours-is-all-you-need-to-achieve-success/

Quotespedia. (n.d.). *A goal without a plan is just a wish.* - Antoine de Saint-Exupéry. https://www.quotespedia.org/authors/a/antoine-de-saint-exupery/a-goal-without-a-plan-is-just-a-wish-antoine-de-saint-exupery/

Remoreras, G. (2011, January 12). *What prioritization and planning can do for you.* #Perspectives. https://glennremoreras.com/2011/01/12/prioritization/

Ripley, S. (2022, August 2). *Planning quotes to take control of your life.* Everyday Power. https://everydaypower.com/planning-quotes/

Rodrigues, D. (2016, August 29). *Why the right mindset matters in planning.* Debbie Rodrigues. https://debbieinshape.com/right-mindset-planning/

SkillPacks. (2020, May 19). *14 growth mindset activities for adults to explore!* https://www.skillpacks.com/growth-mindset-activities/

Succedict. (2020, May 20). *35 execution quotes to inspire you to execute.* https://succedict.com/quotes-on-execution/

Tardi, C. (2019). *How to apply the 80-20 rule.* Investopedia. https://www.investopedia.com/terms/1/80-20-rule.asp

The Logical Indian. (2015, June 5). *Inspirational success story of Sylvester Stallone: Rags to riches.* https://thelogicalindian.com/story-feed/get-inspired/inspirational-success-story-of-sylvester-stallone-rags-to-riches/

Timeular. (2022, July 23). *What are time wasters at work and how to avoid them?* https://timeular.com/blog/time-wasters-work/

Valamis. (2022, February 17). *Continuous learning.* https://www.valamis.com/hub/continuous-learning

ABOUT THE AUTHOR

Michael Wu, a multifaceted entrepreneur, venture capitalist, and bestselling author, renowned for his work in fostering innovation and entrepreneurship. With a Master's degree from HEC Paris, Michael first cut his teeth in the corporate world, spending a decade in management consulting and venture capital, and culminating as the Vice President of a boutique investment firm in Vancouver.

Embarking on his entrepreneurial journey in 2015, Michael has since navigated various online business models, including e-commerce, affiliate marketing, agency, courses, and more. His hands-on experience and business acumen have led to the establishment of his multi 8-figure online business empire, a testament to his unwavering determination and innovative spirit.

Michael's myriad accomplishments include achieving many #1 Best Sellers on Amazon and penning several bestselling books. His story is one of resilience and perseverance, having immigrated at the age of 29 to a new country where he was a stranger to all, a challenge that propelled him out of his comfort zone and into a journey of discovery and continuous learning.

Driven by a mission to enlighten others on the boundless possibilities of the online business world, Michael strives to help individuals attain the freedom, independence, and life they desire. His approach is one of sincerity and commitment, emphasizing that while the road to success demands hard work, the rewards are profoundly fulfilling.

Michael invites readers and aspiring entrepreneurs to delve deeper into the realms of digital entrepreneurship through his website: www.PageOneFormula.com. In his writings and teachings, he shares not just practical insights and strategies, but also a vision of empowerment and independence that has transformed his own life.

Printed in Great Britain
by Amazon

38866448R00126